A MIRACLE JOURNEY

Elly Stone

A Miracle Journey

Typeset in Times New Roman

A Miracle Journey: memoir
ISBN 978-1-4461-1590-9

Printed, bound and published by *Lulu.com*
www.lulu.com

DEDICATION

I have written this book in dedication to
my amazing sister, Helen, who died age 38

CONTENTS

ACKNOWLEDGEMENTS

I would like to acknowledge the generous assistance given to me as I worked on my life story project.

- The SA Writers' Centre – Thanks for all the support you have given me over the past two years, especially Jude, Malcolm, and the Richard Llewelyn Arts and Disability Trust Fund.
- Novita Children's Services (formerly the Crippled Children's Association of SA) – For information about Cerebral Palsy and access to archives.
- Mike Bull – Thanks for suggesting that I write this book, otherwise I would never have written it. Thanks for all the support you have given me.
- Ray Tyndale – Thanks for helping me by proofreading my story.
- Jill Chapman, MOSH (Minimisation of Suicide Harm – For your commitment and dedication to the support of those bereaved through suicide
- And thanks to all the others who have helped me in this project – I am so grateful.

FOREWORD

Told from a personal point of view, this true story relates the life of a woman who grew up with Cerebral Palsy and suffered various forms of abuse, yet overcame her debility and fought to improve her life.

For over thirty years Elly blocked out the pain and traumatic abuse she suffered at the hands of her father and her brother. Remembering these difficult times and recording her thoughts and feelings were not easy. She found some solace in writing poems about the times of abuse. In letters that were never sent she told the abusers how she felt, and what she remembered. This was the only way she could bring her emotions out and cope with revealing untold truths that had remained a secret between Elly and her sister.

To overcome the successive deaths of her loved ones, including her mother, sister and her husband, Elly again took pen to paper and wrote letters to them, telling them how she felt about their deaths. Now she has written her story: a story of a woman's struggle, but also of her determination and fighting spirit. She did what she had to do to rise above the setbacks. Words from the past join with recent recollections, to capture Elly's hope and loss. At times funny, at times heart-wrenching, the story also seeks to inform the reader. It is a story of disability, of family, of a haunting and tormenting past, and of a search for happiness and peace.

One

MY EARLY YEARS

Born at the Queen Victoria Hospital to Grace and Charles Thompson, I was the youngest of eight children, five boys and three girls. My entrance into this world wasn't an easy one. Mum had difficulty giving birth because I was breach. The doctors tried to turn me; when they couldn't they decided to act quickly as they were losing both my mother and me. The doctors and nurses had to take me away quickly into a humidicrib because I was slipping fast. I had tubes all over my little body. While I was in the humidicrib I nearly died three times. The doctors and the nurses named me *"The Miracle Baby"* because I kept fighting to stay alive and would not give up.

Soon after I was born, the hospital staff noticed something wrong with my legs. My feet were turned in towards each other. The doctors decided that I had cerebral palsy. During my first year of life I had many operations, mainly to try to fix my legs. This was just the beginning of countless operations and treatments throughout the rest of my life. I spent most of my first year in hospital and on machines.

It was considered that I only had a mild case of cerebral palsy called Spastic Cerebral Palsy. This is the most common type. I had stiffness and tightness of the muscles in both legs. This made movement difficult or even impossible. Cerebral palsy stopped me from walking until I was two and a half years old. I also suffered epileptic fits for most of my childhood. The seizures isolated me from other people because, in those days, people with epilepsy were feared. People tended to shun them rather than give them the friendship and empathy they needed. Fortunately I grew out of the epilepsy during my young married life.

When I was about three years old, the doctors decided to try callipers to help me walk and to try to improve my muscles. At first I was scared of these strange-looking devices that were strapped below my knees. But my mother made it better. She explained that I needed to wear the callipers to make me walk better. Mum would let me dress up my teddy bear and put the callipers on her. We called the teddy "Pooh Bear". To this day I still have and love Pooh Bear. To help me feel better, Mum would tuck me into bed and bring my pet rabbit for me until I went to sleep.

My mother was a kind, loving and diligent working class woman. Born in the Riverland, she met my dad at their work and, against her parents' wishes, married him at the age of 21. During their married life and my childhood, they moved house many times, often to country areas and metropolitan Adelaide, in order for Dad to get work. In those days there was an endowment payment, which was only 2 pounds a month for the first child. This payment went up a little with every child that followed. Mother received a cheque in the post each month. She would have to pay for clothes and shoes for us children out of the payment. If she had anything left, she would buy us a surprise to share. Back then a few pence got all of us a packet of lollies at the local corner shop.

When I was about eight years old my mother bought me my first purse. I was delighted to have my own purse – my eyes lit up with excitement. I wanted to be all grown up like my sisters. When I opened the purse I discovered the first money I every owned, as my mother had put in a sixpence. Mum always said you would never be broke if you kept a sixpence in your purse. To this day, I still keep 5 cents in my purse, knowing Mum would be checking on me if she were still alive.

My dad was about five years older than my mother. He was a boilermaker for the best part of his younger life. This allowed him to work as a fireman on the steam trains. My eldest brother also worked on the trains and he would take me for free on the train into town. We would sit in the front seat so I could look out the window, as I wanted to see everything. When I saw any animals such as sheep or cows I would get excited and scream out. All the other people on the train would give me a smile.

Due to the cerebral palsy, my parents were very wary about how I was treated. They cuddled me a lot, and watched how my brothers and sisters interacted with me. I was isolated from my family due to the constant trips to the Children's' Hospital, where I was regularly treated with speech therapy, physiotherapy and leg operations. This caused stress and strain in the whole family. When we lived in the country, there was a lot of travel to Adelaide for appointments. Mum would come with me but she worried about the other children back home. It was hard for my mother to cope, but she did somehow.

I remember one time having to catch a train from Jamestown to go to my hospital appointments. Another time my brother, James, came along and was supposed to take me to my treatment while Mum did some errands in the city. Instead my brother took me to the River Torrens to see the ducks and gave me a ride on the tour boat "The Popeye". When Mum came to find me at the hospital, I wasn't there. She was terrified that something awful had happened to my brother and me. When finally we returned, my mother asked where we'd been. I dobbed my brother in by saying, "Ducks, Mum. Ducks. Popeye."

I was not close to all my siblings. Most of the time we fought like cats and dogs, just as most kids do. My oldest sister thought she was the black sheep of the family. Mum made her do most of the chores around the house. Everybody thought I was the favourite because of how much attention and care I needed and because I was the baby. Because I was the youngest, my brothers and sisters would do stuff and blame it all on me so I would get into trouble instead of them. Before I was born, my oldest brother Michael bought me a panda bear, a koala bear and a train set, thinking that I would be a boy. I kept those toys for years; I didn't want to get rid of them because my brother gave them to me. I still have the panda bear. However, my mother ended up selling the train set without telling me. The koala bear lost most of its fur and I got rid of it after I was married.

I believe my brother was a little disappointed that I was not a boy but he was proud of me anyway. My relationship with Michael was an excellent one. I was so close to him and we did a lot together. My sister Helen and I also got along really well; she used to stick up for me against the others. She would help Mum to dress me and get me ready for my appointments. She read me stories if Mum couldn't. Both Michael and Helen were my protectors when things happened in my life.

I grew up in a three-bedroom house. Being a family of ten we had to share bedrooms because there were so many of us. There wasn't much space to go around - the three girls were in one bedroom, and the five boys in another. Mum washed our clothes in an old Pope clothes washer with a wringer. She heated the water and boiled the white washing in a large copper. She lit a fire under the copper and stirred the clothes with a large stick, like a thick broom handle. Doing the washing took her hours and hours of hard work. The washing was rinsed in troughs and put through the wringer before hanging it on lines strung across the back yard. I would join mother while she was washing and talk my head off, saying anything that popped into my mind. To keep me quiet, mum would ask me to hold the sheets while she put them in the wringer in case they got stuck. Mum would also sweep the floors and then get on her hands and knees to wash and polish them.

When it was time to iron the clothes, Mum used the kitchen table as an ironing board. She would put an old blanket at the end of the table then a white sheet over the blanket. Then she would get a bowl of water and use a wet rag to spray the clothes. However, Mum had to stop doing household chores because she became too ill. This got her down because she couldn't do what she wanted to do. Finally Helen decided to take Mum to the doctor. The tests showed that she had cancer. She was only sixty-one, too young, when she became sick. She never stopped fighting the illness until the end. In a way, Mum and I were the same – we both were "battlers". Eventually, the cancer took Mum's strength and she couldn't do much at all. she just rested and stayed in bed most of the time.

Mum always loved her footie. When Port Adelaide was playing on a Saturday afternoon she would get the radio, a pot of tea, some "ciggies" and her knitting, ready to listen to the game. When the quarter was over she would boil the kettle on the stove and then add more water to the pot. The tea was extremely strong, as she would put enough in each morning to last most of the day. While the football was on, nobody could talk or do anything. Mum was not to be disturbed. If Port lost, Mum would blame the umpires every time, she was a one-eyed Port supporter.

I remember every Sunday, Mum would get up early to start preparing the meat for the roast lunch. We always had lamb for Sunday lunch with roast potatoes, roast carrots, peas and cauliflower with home-made gravy. This was followed by sweets for desserts like pudding and hot custard, or bread and butter pudding, or rice cream custard. After lunch we would go and watch TV together or play games.

When I was old enough, my oldest brother and I would go to Melbourne every Christmas for a week. We did this for about five years. We would start a "Christmas Club" at the beginning of the year until November. We used to catch the Overland in the evening and travel all night, arriving in Melbourne at 8.00am. It took around 10 hours to get there and we kept ourselves entertained by playing cards and eating chips. We would book a place in Fitzroy and stay for a week. We would have a day on a bus trip to Phillip Island to see the penguins. I loved going there to watch the penguins come in from the sea and waddle to their burrows. Our treat was to buy dinner, at the fish and chips shop. Then we would go back to the penguins to eat. A lot of seagulls would come. I always felt sorry for them, so would throw pieces of chips for them to squawk and fight over.

I was around eight when we started going to my Auntie Emily's place. Mum was the youngest of eight children; Auntie Emily was her third oldest sister. We usually went on a Sunday morning and would get up early to leave. Most times it was Mum, Michael and I that went but sometimes Paul and Jack came too.

We would catch a bus into the city, then take the tram to Glenelg before walking the rest of the way to my auntie's place. While we were walking, mum used to warn us all to behave while we were there because she knew what her sister was like. My auntie was very strict. She didn't like anyone touching her precious photographs, ornaments and figurines – she didn't want anything to get broken. Mum used to say, "Just talk when you're spoken to, don't ask for anything, don't touch anything and don't run around!" She also told us to not let Auntie Emily know that Mum was smoking. Mum hid her smoking habit from her sisters and brothers for years. However, they all knew that she was a smoker – you could smell the smoke on her clothes and her fingertips were yellow. But the others never let on that they knew and Mum went to her grave keeping this "secret".

I enjoyed going to my auntie's place because she used to cook delicious things that my mum never made. She was a very good cook and made cakes and biscuits from scratch. Everyone loved her food and we gave her the nickname of "Auntie Cook". Another distinctive feature of Auntie Emily was her hairstyle. She wore her hair the same way for as long as I can remember. Her hair always was put up in a bun at the back and to keep it neat and in place, she wore a hair net and about a half dozen hair clips. Even when Auntie Emily went to parties and family gatherings, her hair was always the same.

I kept in touch with Auntie Emily by ringing her every week and I visited her when I could. She died at the age of 103.

Until her death, she remained remarkably active and lived on her own until she broke her hip a few months before she died. She continued to play lawn balls three times a week and go on outings with a seniors group. The last time I saw her I was amazed that she was still cooking three meals a day. And she was buried with her hair in the same style!

Every year we went to the Wayville Showgrounds for the Royal Adelaide Show, which was held in the September school holidays. For weeks, I would save up all the pocket money Mum gave me so I could spend it on rides and show bags. My brother Michael worked selling newspapers and he let me help him as the Show approached so I could earn extra spending money. My job was to hand out papers while Michael took the money and chatted with his regular customers. There were two places where we worked: in front of Adelaide train station (near the famous Adelaide pie cart) and at the corner of Rundle Mall and King William Street, next to Ernsmith's appliance store. I didn't really earn that much money for my efforts but it all helped in building up my funds for the Show.

We would spend the whole day at the Show. When we arrived, the first thing we did was go to the show bag pavilion. During the year I wasn't allowed to buy chocolate or lollies but at Showtime Mum gave me permission to buy ten show bags. I would have bought more but ten was the limit! Mum let me choose my show bags and I would pick the ones with lots of lollies in them. Every year I got the same ten bags - Bertie Beetle, Kit Kat, Snakes Alive, Violet Crumble, Red Skins, Milky Bars, Smarties, Minties, Freddo Frog and finally Cadburys. My brothers in particular would try to "con" me by trading things they didn't like in their bags for better things from my bags. Sometimes I fell for this, but not very often. I tried to make my treasured treats last as long as possible.

Next we would walk around the grounds to see what else we could see. I wanted to go on the rides but Mum was very careful about which ones were suitable for a young girl with a disability. Rides I wanted to go on were the Ferris wheel, chair lift, the Big Dipper, Ghost Train, Gee Whiz, the Cha Cha, and the Mad Mouse. Mum wasn't very keen on many of these rides. There was a big "NO!" for the Mad Mouse - Mum was determined that I wasn't going on that one. I was upset with her but when she was off on her own for a few minutes, Michael said that he would take me on the Mad Mouse without her knowing. My brothers and sister got her away for a while and Michael and I lined up for the forbidden ride. After I had finished, I knew why Mum had said no. I was so scared when I was going up and down and around. When I got off the ride, I was white as a ghost. And to make things worse, I threw up! When Mum returned she knew something was wrong and we had to confess what we'd done. She was not at all happy.

Fortunately for me, Michael got most of the blame for our misadventure.

For the rest of the day we would see what else we could find around the showgrounds. There was a farmyard nursery with calves, lambs, chickens, ponies, puppies and baby goats. We saw exhibitions and attractions like the wood chopping, delicate handicraft, arts, and cookery. And there were a lot of different foods like buckets of chips, Dagwood dogs on sticks, hot potatoes, fairy floss and ice creams. The day finished with a big fireworks show at the grandstand. By the time we got home, it was almost midnight. The day at the Show was always special.

When I was around sixteen, I told my mum that I wanted to start smoking like her and the other children. My mother told me that I could but there was a big "BUT". She told me "Do not ask me for smokes or money to buy them". I decided not to start up smoking after all. Mother knew I wouldn't, that's why she said that.

Mum's efforts to keep her children on the straight and narrow were not always this successful. My youngest brother Jack was turning out to be a bit of a handful, somewhat of a "wild boy". By the age of 15, he had dropped out of school after being hit by a car in front of our house and suffering a major head injury.

But he also stayed out late at night, leaving Mum waiting and wondering where he was. In reality what he was doing was stealing and breaking and entering. Jack wound up doing time in jail on more than one occasion and Mum would visit him every Sunday. Most times Mum forced me to come along. Jack was not my favourite brother and I would rather have stayed at home. But off we would go on the bus, arriving at the city jail and walking down the long narrow path to the prison building. After signing in, we had to wait to be called for our visit. Any items for my brother had to be left with the guards, who seemed to be everywhere, opening and closing gates and asking us who we were there to visit. Eventually, we got to the prisoners' visiting area. Jack and the other prisoners each were already seated in their small cubicle, where thick glass separated them from their visitors. Mum and Jack did most of the talking; my brother and I would barely say hello. After our 20 minutes of visiting time, Mum and I left and caught the bus back home. At least I had Mum's Sunday roast lunch to look forward to.

I can recall the first time that I was old enough to vote. Mum always advised me to vote Labor, as they were the party for the working man. It was because of Dad working that mother said this. Labor would give us more money than the Libs, who were only for big business. On voting day Mum and I went to the local school and got our names checked on the electoral roll.

Mum voted first then she came over to where I was preparing to fill in the ballot, leaning over my shoulder; she stood behind me to make sure I voted Labor. And I did.

As I got older, though, I had to start making more of my own decisions. When I was eighteen I was at the dental hospital to have my wisdom teeth examined. While I was waiting I started to have pain in my left side. The pains had actually been going on for a week or so. The pain was getting worse as I sat in the dentist's chair. When I was finished, I decided I better go to the outpatients department around the corner. I didn't have long to wait. The first doctor who saw me wasn't sure what was going on. So he called another physician for his advice. He didn't know either. Then a surgeon came to see me and he picked up what was wrong. It was my appendix. They needed to operate straight away, as the appendix was ready to rupture. In those days it was dangerous not to take your appendix out. After all my times in the hospital, this was the first operation that I had to sign for on my own. When Mum came home from work she asked the boys where I was - nobody knew. Mum got worried – had I been in an accident, or something else terrible? She rang the hospital and found out I was in theatre having my appendix out.

My childhood was a blur of hospital visits. I lived most of my first year of life in hospital care.

Before I started attending school, and after I had had operations on my legs, I would go to stay at Somerton, a rehabilitation centre run by the Children's Hospital for children with disabilities. Mum used to visit at weekends. I liked Somerton because I got to meet other kids with disabilities and I made new friends. I kept in contact with some for many years after. I remember two friends in particular, Bernice and Kathleen. Bernice was a tall Aboriginal girl with very black hair whose family was from Alice Springs. Because Bernice had polio, her legs were affected like mine and she needed braces too. Kathleen was younger than Bernice and me, but we all got along really well. Kathleen had long blond hair and a pretty face, and her cheeky grin allowed her to get away with things that the rest of us couldn't. One of the nurses, Robyn, would sometimes take Bernice, Kathleen and me out for special occasions away from Somerton. We would go to the movies, or for a picnic, or to visit Robyn's mother. Robyn's mum had a big back garden where we would have lunch or morning tea. The first movie we went to was *Mary Poppins* and we also saw *The Sound of Music*. We always tried to be on our best behaviour when we went out with Robyn. She had an old car and I always sat in the front seat beside her. Years later, Robyn told me that I was her favourite. Robyn became a very good friend whom I have known now for forty-eight years. Although she now lives in New Zealand, we still correspond, talk on the phone and meet up occasionally when she is "back in town". She even paid for me to visit her four times in New Zealand. She has been like a guardian angel taking care of an innocent.

Sometimes I'd stay in Estcourt House where children with cerebral palsy were cared for. In charge was Matron Smyth who spent 11 years at Estcourt House. There were three wards - a baby ward, and separate wards for boys and girls. The staff included physiotherapists, domestics and people from the Education Department. While I was at Estcourt House they got better physiotherapy equipment and air-conditioning in all the wards. There were four TV sets supplied to each of the wards. The TVs were bigger than the small black and white TV we had at home. The children didn't have anywhere for relaxation so we ate, slept and played in the wards. Later a recreation room was built. It was called Edwards Recreation Room. We were sometimes taken in staff cars to things such as John Martin's Christmas Pageant, to see the ships in Port Adelaide or down to the beach at Semaphore. Mr Thompson made all the leg splints at Estcourt House in the old stables that had been converted to a workshop.

When I began school, I went to Ashford Special School on Anzac Highway. It is still there now. Miss Gum was the

Principal and my first teacher was Miss Bagshaw. They were caring and patient people. There were up to ten children in a class and the teachers had assistants who were studying to become teachers themselves. The school provided extra help to children with learning difficulties. They gave us tuition to bring us up to normal class standards. I eventually made it to a regular school and attended Years 5-7 there, followed by a year in technical school. After I was married, Miss Gum and Miss Bagshaw came to visit me while I was living out in the bush. Even though I had kept in touch by phone with Miss Gum after leaving Ashford, when they arrived unexpectedly, Miss Gum must have seen the puzzled look on my face and said "You don't recognise us, do you?" I didn't, until they spoke! We spent time catching up and telling stories about times at Ashford School.

My regular treatments, such as physiotherapy, were organised by the Crippled Children's Association. Every year I attended a camp at Oakbank Racecourse with the Girl Guides, called the Crippled Children's Camps and later the Edna Ayers Camps. These were held during the Christmas holidays in January. Mother and I would catch a bus into town to meet with all the other campers at the Crippled Children's Association building on Franklin Street. Once everyone was there we would go to Oakbank by bus. When we arrived all the Girl Guides would help everyone off the bus and pair us to the Guides who would be our companions and look after us while we were there. There was a Girl Guide for every child with a disability attending the camp.

We used to stay in tents, have campfires and toast marshmallows, as well as do other fun activities, like campfire singsongs, dressing-ups, performing in skits, and making things. We would go to a property that was owned by a Mr Kemp. We had barbecues there and Mr Kemp let us go in his swimming pool. On one of the days at camp, the Police Greys (a group of about ten police horses) came up and we were given rides around the campsite. On another occasion we travelled to Mannum on the River Murray and went for a ride and a meal on the paddle steamer *"Avoca"*.

The meals at the Oakbank camp were held in a large room under the grandstand. Some of the Girl Guides were rostered to help in the kitchen. Others served meals and helped the children to eat. Early in the mornings from the grandstand we could see the jockeys training the horses. The training went on every morning of the camp. The horses were timed to see how they were progressing, and some horses were racing each other.

It was great to get away from the treatments at hospital, and I met new friends. Over the years, I have maintained contact with some of the Guides – Lorraine, Margaret and Gillian - who were my companions at camp. These people remained special friends from those times at Oakbank.

I stayed at Ashford Special School until Grade Five, then went to Hindmarsh Primary School to finish my primary schooling. After that I went to Thebarton Technical School for a year and left when I was fifteen. My grades weren't that good and because my schooling was delayed by illness and treatments, I was the oldest in my class. I felt different to the other girls. Kids teased me because of my disability. They used to call me "spastic" and stare at me. When I told my mum, she said I should stand up for myself and tell them "Take a picture, it will last longer!" On days when I had the guts, I did what she'd suggested. After that, the other kids respected me more for who I was and teased me less. But in the end, I just wanted to leave. When I told Mum what I was planning, she hit the roof! She tried to talk me into staying but I held my ground – I knew I was old enough to leave school. Later I became a mature age student and did my SACE in my late 30s and early 40s, after I was married. My husband had mixed feelings about me studying – on the one hand, he was proud of me (he left school at 13 to help his dad) but on the other, he did not want me "getting smarter" than him. I am still doing courses because it helps me keep my mind occupied.

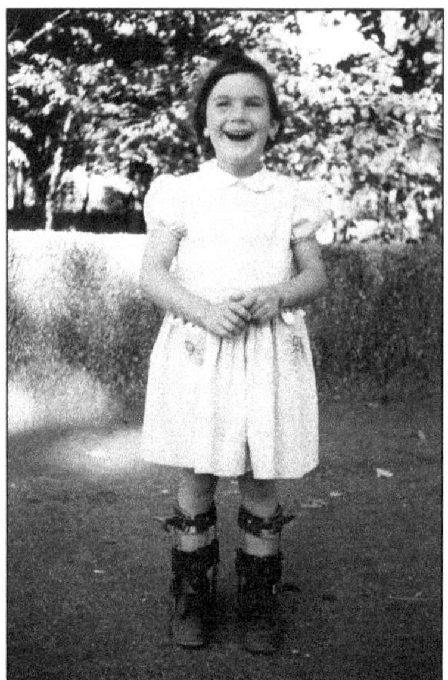

My early years (approximately age 5-6)

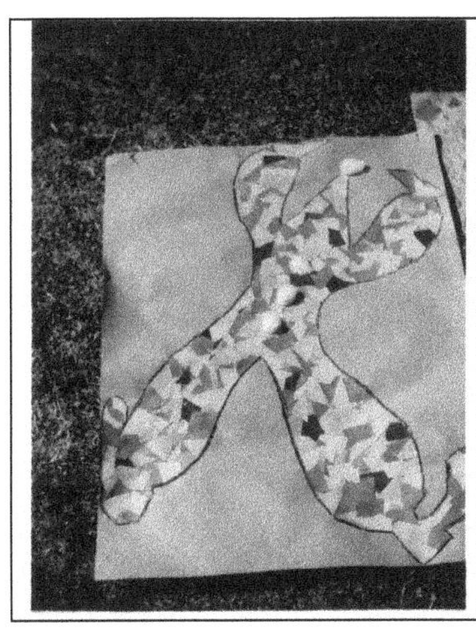

Top: Tents at Oakbank Girl Guide Camp

Middle: Entering the dining area under the Oakbank grandstand

Bottom: Some craft work

A day trip on the Showboat Avoca,
part of the Oakbank Camp

Estcourt House, Grange, South Australia

Two

MY TRIP

The year I was twenty, I wanted to do something very different in my life. After much thought I decided to go on a cruise. It was the opportunity of a lifetime, a chance to meet some of my pen pals, whom I'd been writing to since I was in school.

I started to check newspapers and visit travel agents. Then I spotted the one I wanted. It was with the ship Fairsky and it was cheap for the ports that they were offering: Darwin, Singapore, Jakarta, Bali and back to Darwin.

I rang P&O cruises to find out more about what I needed to do to book the cruise. I was interested in going on a cruise that I had thought about for a long time and was saving up for. I had to try to make arrangements for somebody to take me to and from the airports. After some ringing around I found a lady from the Salvation Army who would help.

I booked the trip before I told mother. Now I had to convince her to let me go. She was very protective and she didn't want me to do anything that would put me in danger. She tried her hardest to talk me out of going, but I'd made up my mind and nothing was going to change it. She was worried because I was going on the ship alone. I needed to do this to prove to her I could look after myself.

I only had six weeks before the ship left on 12 June 1977. I had a lot to organise before I left. The lady from the Salvation Army rang me with the name of the person who was meeting me in Darwin. I would stay with her until the Fairsky sailed on the night of the 12th. She also arranged a couple to take me to the airport.

The night before I was due to go I couldn't sleep, I was too excited. Mother stayed up with me until they came to pick me up at 5:00am. Mother held back her tears until I drove off. When we arrived at the airport it was only around thirty minutes before I was due to get on the plane to Darwin International Airport. The couple stayed with me until I was safely on the plane.

When the plane took off, we had three-and-half hours in the air. The flight attendants were very good with me and all the other passengers. When we landed at Darwin airport the lady was there to meet me. She had a Salvation Army uniform on. Her name was Ruth and she was tall, with dark hair, in her late forties. I stayed with her for the rest of the day and night until 10:00pm when I had to board the ship.

Ruth showed me around Darwin including places where Cyclone Tracy had hit. She told me what the government was doing to make Darwin a better place after Tracy. They were replacing all the buildings and spreading out more than before. Central Darwin near the wharf was now high-rise, which she felt had spoilt the old city. Darwin has spread out south to the city of Palmerston and many people live on 5-acre blocks. At Robertson Barracks are the houses for soldiers. There are still the old folks who were living there when Tracy hit. They live in Darwin on 5 and 20-acre blocks beyond Palmerston such as Howard Springs, Humpty Doo or Berry Springs.

Ruth took me to church that night and they had a spread on afterwards. Everyone was friendly and wanted to know about me. We went to the harbour around 9:00pm. The ship was all lit up - it looked beautiful. A lot of people were already on board. I said my goodbyes and boarded the ship, and Ruth and her husband Frank waited there until the ship left the harbour.

When we left, the ship's horn blew and everyone was waving madly to his or her families and friends. The ship sailed slowly out of the harbour and you could hear the waves hitting the side of the ship.

We all found our cabins. I was sharing with another lady, who was older than me. She was tall with grey hair. She helped me find our way to the dining room, lido bar, cinema, and the grand social room. She helped me at other times too.

The first seaport we stopped at was Singapore. As we arrived many people stood on the wharf holding signs with people's names. My pen pals had a big sign with my name in the middle of it in black. It stood out very clearly. When we came into the wharf there was a clanging of chains and traffic noise, different from the ship's peaceful tranquillity while sailing.

When I came ashore I was surprised how most people couldn't speak English. I looked different to people around me with my skin colour, and my limited knowledge of the world.

My friends Nancy and Kim showed me around Singapore. They drove me to where they lived then showed me their houses. Most houses were multi-story and very close to other houses. I hadn't seen this kind of housing before. We ate some fish and rice. Nancy suggested we see Sri Mariamman

Temple, Singapore's oldest Hindu temple dating back to the 18th century. It is used for the fire walking festival Thimithi and is the preferred venue of Hindu weddings. As you enter the gates you look up at the tower over the entrance of the temple. It's covered with figurative sculptures of gods and goddesses and mythological beasts.

This tower is visible from a distance so people can say their prayers without stepping inside the temple. There are strings of mango and coconut leaves hanging above the temple doors, signs of welcome and purity. Before you enter the temple you must remove your shoes and leave them outside. You are required to ring the bell before entering, then you must purify by washing your hands and feet and sprinkling water on other people's heads. After doing all this you walk in a clock-wise direction and encircle the temple hall an odd number of times; this is a sign of good luck.

Afterwards, we went into another room where everyone prayed. There were dozens on the floor praying to gods. They do this for hours, and then they have lunch and go back to praying. It was amazing to see how people from another culture behave.

It was getting late and I needed to go back to the ship. It had been a long day with Nancy and Kim and I enjoyed my time with them. On the way back to the ship we arranged to meet the next day to go to Chinatown to shop for gifts for my friends back home. I was too tired to go out to party with my cabin mate so I had an early night. I didn't even hear her come in for the night.

I woke up early and showered and dressed before my cabin mate woke up. After breakfast Nancy and Kim arrived and we drove to Chinatown. It was busy with cars and bikes on the roads as people were going to work, as if everyone wanted to be first to get to where they were going.

Chinatown was behind skyscrapers in Singapore's financial district. There were Chinese merchants engaging in businesses from ground floor to shop houses. I experienced the sights and sounds of Chinatown by walking around smelling herbs and spices and other exotic ingredients, seeing traditional delicacies like sea cucumbers drying in the streets, fruit sellers, and fortune-tellers sitting at tables eagerly awaiting customers. There was a lot of noise. I had never experienced this atmosphere before. I saw people bartering prices.

There also were bargains, from beautiful embroidered kimonos, gold jewellery and t-shirts to pottery and traditional crafts at hard-to-believe prices. At the Tanjong Pagar area there were traditional teashops, clog and kite makers, painted masks, waxed paper umbrellas. You could get delicious local food such as eels, turtles and catfish at very affordable prices.

Tired of walking around we hired a rickshaw. It felt so good not to walk the rest of Chinatown. We were only half way around. The rickshaw man was about 65 with grey hair and not much English. It was different travelling around this way. The driver didn't care about anyone else, he just peddled. When someone got in his way he would just peddle faster to see who would win.

I enjoyed every part of Chinatown. On the way back to the ship we stopped to eat. Nancy and Kim were hungry but I wasn't so I just had a small amount. I wasn't used to eating this kind of food. Some of the food I'd seen at the markets put me off eating.

The ship was lit up. You could hear everyone having a good time on board, singing, dancing, drinking and laughing, with music playing. Nancy and Kim made sure I was on board the ship before they left.

In the morning they wanted to come back as we sailed for Jakarta. They arrived early to make sure that they didn't miss me, and brought me a gift to remind me of our time together.

We said our goodbyes and I thanked them for showing me around. It was a sad to be leaving two good friends.

The Fairsky pulled out slowly. The captain blew the horn loudly. We sailed away then it was quiet again compared with Singapore. Singapore was a crazy place where nobody sat still for long in one place. On the ship you could take your time getting where you wanted to go.

The Fairsky had dress up themes at night in the grand social room. One night was a Country and Western, another night Rock and Roll, then a Hawaiian theme.

It was hot and humid, but very different from Singapore. While we were at sea the air was clean, no fuel pollution, just the smell of seaweed and salt. At night the sky was clear and star filled. It was beautiful to see.

We had a whole day in Jakarta. My roommate and I made arrangements to stay together. Again, I saw a different side of how people live compared to Australia.

We saw meat hanging in the open with flies all around. Dirty water and sewage running down the gutters and people washing their clothes in toilets. We were afraid to eat anything in case we got sick. Most of us were glad to be back on the ship that evening. Seeing a place like Jakarta and witnessing how most people lived was an eye opener.

After we started to sail away most of us were tired and glad to be leaving. An hour or so after we set sail I decided to call it a night. I took a sleeping pill then went to bed. I was sound asleep when my friend came in for the night.

It was not long after that I was awakened abruptly by my roommate shouting and shaking me. When I looked around, I could see water pouring into our cabin from the outside wall. The ship had struck an uncharted submerged wreck and the hole was on D Deck, right where my cabin was. Finally awake, I knew I had to leave quickly. My roommate had been frightened that she wouldn't be able to wake me up and get me up the stairs.

When we opened the cabin door we saw the crew helping the passengers. Everyone was running around trying to get up the stairs. My friend was trying to help me but I fell a few times, trying my hardest to get where we had to go. My legs wouldn't move quickly and I felt that I wouldn't be able to make it out. I was thinking that my time was up. But my friend wouldn't give up on me. She made sure I was safe.

On the top deck many of passengers were panicking, shouting and frantically asking questions about what had happened. Fortunately it was a warm tropical night, as we were just in our nightclothes – we hadn't had time to take anything as we fled from our cabin. The crew was good to us and we were given life jackets. About 100 people had lost all their belongings and were the first to go on the lifeboats. The ship was partially sunk and was on a 30-degree angle. Thirty-one cabins were flooded beneath the waterline. My roommate and I were helped into a small lifeboat that held around 6 people. We were all in shock and just followed instructions. A crewmember was with us as the lifeboat was lowered into the sea.

We headed back to Jakarta, propelled by the small motor in the lifeboat. I could see the front of the ship sticking out of the water and it hit me that I was lucky to be alive. The captain had radioed Jakarta that passengers were returning and people were waiting at the docks to assist us. We were put in a motel and given two hundred dollars to go shopping to buy some clothes. When they gave us the money, they arranged for local people to help us. It was hard to buy clothes as Indonesians are generally shorter and their clothes were made differently to ours. When we saw the motel we were surprised, as we hadn't seen that motel the day we spent in Jakarta. It was a tall building with a lot of rooms. The rooms were very pleasant. The people who worked there were good to everyone.

While this was happening there was a plane strike, so we had to stay in the motel for a couple of days. Arrangements were made with the airlines for a special flight to get us back to Australia as soon as possible. In the end, we had to fly to Melbourne and then take the train to Adelaide.

Mother didn't hear about what was happening to me. She was getting ready to go down the street, as it was payday and shopping day. She lined up at the bank and got her money out. After she received her money, she would always do the grocery shopping first, and then buy the vegetables. Then she would go to the butcher. In those days if you wanted to know what was going on you just had to ask a butcher.

When Mum went into the butcher's the owner asked her what ship I was on. Mother was not sure of its name. He told her about the wreck. She ran out of the butcher's and hailed the next taxi home. When she went inside Mum told my older brother and then rang the cruise office. They confirmed it was the ship I was on.

She was worried about how I was coping, being on my own. She was trying to ring the motel where we were all staying but couldn't get an answer. I was trying to contact her but I couldn't get through either. When we finally did talk all she could say was "I told you it was not good to go!"

When we arrived back there was a newspaper person wanting to interview someone from the ship. They saw my friend and asked to interview us. Then I saw Mum at the station. We cried and hugged each other. She said that I wasn't going on any more holidays alone! Then we went home. The next day's Advertiser included the story "SA girl in drama as ship holed".

SS Fairsky, sunk June 1977

Top: Bar and lounge, SS Fairsky

Middle: Dining room, SS Fairsky

Bottom: Two-bed cabin, SS Fairsky

(Source: http://www.ssmaritime.com/sitmar2.htm)

Sri Mariamman Temple
(Photo by Terence Ong, May 2006)

Chinatown, Singapore

Darwin houses damaged by Cyclone Tracy, Christmas Day 1974
(Source: Wikipedia, photo provided by Billbeee)

House girders twisted during Cyclone Tracy
(Source: Wikipedia, photo provided by Bidgee)

HMAS Arrow beached in Francis Bay during Cyclone Tracy
(Source: Wikipedia, photo provided by Billbeee)

Three

ABUSE

I dealt with the abuse by blocking it out of my mind for over thirty years. There were times when I could put it behind me. But there would be a time when my brother came into my life again. When this happened, I started to have nightmares and flashbacks about the abuse. This scared me, going back and remembering what had happened to me.

There was a long skinny passage that you had to walk up before you got into the room, which was under the house. Dad would take the bits of wood off so we could get down the stairs. A small room, a bed, a tap over an old sink, and no window. It was smelly and there were a lot of spiders' webs that you would hit if you weren't sure where they were. It was creepy and dark. Dad pulled the cord and the light came on. The floor was dirt and we had to be careful where we walked so the dirt wouldn't fly around. It made me sad when I had to go into the room because I knew what was going to happen. I was scared to talk in case I would be in trouble. I asked Dad not to do the things to me, but he wouldn't listen.

The nightmares started when I was in my late 30's, early 40's. I started to remember what had happened to me when I was a little girl. I found out later that these events were true. I actually thought they were just bad dreams and they would go away like dreams do. But they came back stronger every time. I would wake up in a sweat, terrified and confused because I was not sure what was going on and I was afraid to go back to sleep. I had tried hard to put them out of my mind but they would not go away.

There was always a little girl in the dreams. She was frightened of another person, a man who was making her do things that she didn't want to do and who was hurting her. I didn't know why I was having these dreams until some time later, when I realised that this little girl was me and that the other person was my brother. I was beginning to remember what had happened to me while I growing up.

In another dream I was forced to have an abortion.

Then the next memory that surfaced through these nightmares was my brother forcing me to have sex with his mates. I remember all of his friends but only one stands out. He was a tall, skinny, freckle-faced red-haired young man. When these events occurred we would go for a drive. I was put in the back of the car, on the floor. They would be drinking beer and smoking cigarettes. The car was littered with bottles of beer, empty and full, and smelled horribly of smoke.

The places would change every time to make sure that I didn't know where I was. These would be places where there was no one else around to see, such as old rundown buildings or alleyways. Once they took me to a church.

It wouldn't take long to go where they had planned and they'd all get out of the car and stand chatting while I sat on the back seat. Whoever paid the money would have sex with me. He would touch me a lot before having sex.

Another dream was about when I spent a week with my dad after he began to live with my sister. And now I have been having nightmares about my dad and what he did to me in a room at the back of the house where we lived.

When these dreams happened it was as if I was going though all the abuse again and I was that scared girl. As if I had no control over what I was dreaming about. It was terrifying to remember what I had actually gone though and kept repressed all those years.

These dreams affected my life by controlling my mind every day until I had no other choice but to tell my husband the truth about what my brother did to me. I didn't tell him the whole story because I knew what he was going to be like when I told him. I could not carry on alone; I had to say something. I think if my husband had not started to ask me questions about my dreams, I wouldn't have told him and we wouldn't have argued that day. My husband was not well. If I'd known, I would not have opened my mouth. I didn't know that my husband was having trouble with his heart. My husband died not long after.

The dreams turned out to be true stories. When I was dreaming about the abortion, I saw the house where it was performed - the front door, the colour of the walls, the street where it was. When my brother had made me have sex with his mates the vision had showed me how many there were and what all of them were like. My dad used to take me to the musty room with a long skinny passage leading to it, the stairs that went down under the back of the back of the house, the little girl being led by the hand, all of these suppressed elements from my past were horribly real.

When my dad took me down there he would say that I was a naughty girl and I had to be punished. It would happen when nobody else was home. Dad would sexually abuse me every time I went into that room. He would tie my hands to the old bed so I wouldn't be able to run. Then he would do things to me so he could get excited. This happened every time he got me into that room. I remember the look on his face, it was if he was looking straight though me. His eyes seemed to be sticking out of his head. He smelled like someone who'd done a hard day's work. He blamed me by saying why did I turn out to be a beautiful young woman. After he'd finished with me I used to go back to my room and cry quiet whimpering sounds. I wouldn't come out until I knew someone else was home.

Now that I am older and have remembered everything that happened to me, I feel that I am coming to terms with it. I am telling my story about my life in an attempt to help other people to understand that they are not alone. There are people out there who can help them.

I found out about my sister and my dad through sharing a room. My other sister Rosemary had left home. Now it was only Helen and me in the girls' bedroom. A time bomb began to tick.

I was 10 years old; Helen was 16. My dad used to come into our room at night when he thought everyone else in the family was sleeping. The shaft of white that intruded into our dark room as he slowly opened the door, allowing the hallway light to enter, signalled his arrival. Then the door was closed and only Dad's shadowy outline could be seen moving toward Helen's bed. He probably would have been drinking since his arrival home from work, as this was his usual routine.

At first, I thought he was just saying goodnight to Helen. But why didn't he come to say goodnight to me? Gradually I started to realise that something "different" was going on. Our beds were only three feet apart and I could feel Dad's presence in our private space. He would sit on Helen's bed and if she was asleep he would wake her up. Then he would play with her by putting his hand under the sheets and touching her, rubbing his hand up and down her body. Sometimes he got into Helen's bed and did "stuff" to her. He would go on top of her or lay on his side facing her back. Other times he would ask my sister to go on top and do things to him. I didn't understand at that age. It seemed like a game – but one that only Dad and Helen could play.

My dad used to look over to my bed to see if I was asleep. I pretended I was sleeping by having my head under the blanket, but with one eye looking out at my sister's bed. I knew that if Dad found out I was awake I'd be in trouble. In the dark, the only sound was whispering from Helen's bed. Clearly I wasn't to be part of this conversation. What was happening was not meant to include me and I was afraid of being caught. But sometimes my curiosity overtook my fear and I remember looking over at my sister's bed on two occasions. One time I could see a look of disgust on Helen's face. I also saw tears in her eyes. On the other occasion, I saw no expression at all on her face, but it was as if she was saying, "Hurry up and finish".

A few months after Dad started to sexually abuse Helen, my brother Jack walked in on what was happening. He didn't say anything at the time. But it was then that he decided to do the same thing to me. My life would never be the same. I remember clearly the first time Jack approached me. He knew that I would do anything for some extra pocket money, like most other 10-year-olds. And he said it had to be a secret between him and me. My mum was away at work and the house was empty. I was confused by what started to happen –

but in some ways it seemed OK because of what Dad had been doing with Helen.

After that, whenever we were alone in the house, Jack abused me. He would wait until he was sure that no one was likely to come back home, and always kept an eye on the front door from the lounge where he did what he did. Over time, I became more nervous and scared about what was going to happen whenever we were alone in the house. I began to realise that another experience of abuse was inevitable. The anxiety and fear turned into nausea in my stomach. I tried to avoid things by watching TV – maybe this would encourage my brother to just go away. But Jack would not take "no" for an answer. He would say, "If it's good for the old man to do that stuff, it's good for me to do it too". And he'd threaten that I was not to tell a soul about what he was doing. "If you open your mouth, I'll deny everything. They'll believe me, not you. And I'll just make things worse for you." Jack was only 13 but he was the type of person who could get around everyone; he got away with a lot. He knew that I would not tell anyone about what he was doing. And he was right. I didn't open my mouth for over 30 years.

However, there was a time when the secret in our family slipped out. We were sitting around the kitchen table, having tea – there was me, Mum, Helen, Michael, Jack and my dad.

Jack and Dad had been drinking and the drink often led to arguments between the two of them. The argument started off innocently enough. But this time, Dad was giving Jack a hard time about stealing things to sell and get money. Dad called Jack a “criminal”.

The fight got more intense. “At least I don’t go around f...ing my daughter!”

“Don’t be bloody stupid!” Dad immediately replied.

Complete silence filled the room. It was like we had just heard that someone had died. In reality, a part of who we were as a family was now gone.

Helen said to Jack, “You’re wrong!”

I just sat there and didn’t open my mouth. Mum was sitting opposite from me and saw all this happen. Because she was deaf as a poker, I’m not sure she even heard all of what was said. Like me, she didn’t say anything. But I noticed a change in her face. As far as I know, this subject never was spoken of again in our family.

I learnt it was not safe to trust others. The abuse from Jack continued. And when my best friend became involved, things just got worse.

Brenda had been my friend since before Jack started abusing me. Our families knew each other and Brenda would come over and we'd hang out together, talking, watching TV, and playing computer games. As we got older, I felt I could tell Brenda some of my secrets. We talked about private girl things. Eventually I plucked up my courage and shared with Brenda about my crush for an older guy. She promised she would not tell a soul about anything we discussed but I didn't know that she liked my brother. Brenda told Jack about my crush and he started to use it to blackmail me. If I refused, he threatened to tell Mum my secrets. I felt I had no choice but to do whatever he asked me. More and more I felt trapped, like I was locked in a cage. My brother would say, "Remember it will be you who gets into trouble, not me." I was convinced this was true. I was increasingly under Jack's control. I don't know if Brenda ever knew what damage her loose lips caused me.

It was my brother who stole my childhood. He was the one who took my virginity. I was still only 10 the first time Jack raped me. It was always an awful experience. I remember screaming every time. Jack was big for his age and didn't care about whether he hurt me. I was small for my age and more vulnerable because of my disability. Jack could easily overpower me whenever he wanted to have sex. As Mum worked most evenings, and Dad went out drinking, the abuse would happen at least once a week, sometimes more often.

When I was 13, Jack made me pregnant. He then had to do something fast so nobody would find out. My brother knew someone who did backyard abortions so he arranged to get rid of the baby. He took me to a house in Kilburn. To get away without mother knowing, my brother told a story about us going away for a couple of days and Mum agreed to this.

I don't remember much about the abortion but can still clearly picture the house where it took place. Jack led me in the front door, like we were going for a visit. We went through the lounge, down a passageway to a bedroom at the back. There was a bed in the room and some metal instruments to be used for the abortion.

Other than that, I remember little. Later in my life, some memories did come through in nightmares, as described at the beginning of this chapter. The abortion damaged my uterus so badly I had to have a hysterectomy in my early twenties, just after I was married. My brother destroyed my hopes of having children with my husband.

Around age thirteen and a half, my brother forced me to have sex with some of his mates to make him feel big to them. He made them pay money. I felt like a prostitute and a slut. My brother had no right to do this to me. But again he convinced me to stay quiet by saying Mum would be ashamed of her little girl if she knew what I had done. And Jack's manipulation continued to work. As the abuse intensified, so did my sense of guilt. I knew that if Mum ever found out what was happening, she would be devastated. Her image of me as her perfect daughter would be shattered. I hated myself.

And the abuse seemed to follow me everywhere. When my oldest sister Rosemary left home, she moved in with her boyfriend, Richard. Ironically, Richard's brother was the man I would eventually marry. But more of that later. I did not like Richard. He talked a lot about sex, had sex magazines, and owned sex toys purchased at adult shops. When I was about 16, Rosemary asked me to stay with her for a week or two to help out with the three children. From this time Richard began to abuse me. He used to come into my bedroom when my sister was asleep or outside and did the same kinds of things to me as Jack. He used to kiss me all over and suck my breast and feel and touch me all over. Once again, I felt that I had no control of my life. Why was this happening to me? What was wrong with me?

I never talked to Helen about the abuse that we both experienced. I didn't tell her what I had seen in our bedroom at night. My dad continued his abuse. He took Helen everywhere with him, to places nobody else was allowed to go. My mum was in denial about my sister and my dad's actions. She just did not believe anything was happening between Helen and my father. Then Helen became pregnant. My mother and Dad started to fight a lot. The time bomb had exploded.

Mum told my dad to leave and not come back. However, Dad insisted that my sister go with him when he got a place to live. Helen didn't really have any choice. And Mum didn't say anything to try to stop this from happening. When Helen found out she was expecting more than one child, mum decided to sell our family home and use the money to buy another house for Helen and the future grandchildren to live in. Ironically, my dad would move into this house too. In fact, the new house was in the name of Helen and my dad. Mum, Michael and I had to move into a Housing Trust house not far from our old family home. At the time, I was glad to be leaving the place where I was being abused – although it did not end with this move. Thinking back on things now, I feel that Mum should never have sold the house. We no longer had money for things we used to get; instead of buying new clothes, Mum would go to second-hand shops. She wound up having nothing to show for all the years she had worked to support our family.

After the babies were born the doctors found out they had a problem. Like me, they had cerebral palsy and other disabilities. Were they like this because they were my dad's children?

When my sister had the babies, she had to tell the Births, Deaths & Marriages that she did not know who the father of her children was. So the births are recorded as "father unknown". Helen always denied that the children were my dad's. She became pregnant another two times but had to have abortions through the insistence of my father. The secrecy within our family continued.

To my brother Jack

I am writing this to you because I felt that I should. I am going to tell you what I have been going through since you came up on my birthday. Also I want to say to you how I feel about you.

Firstly I would like to say that you have once again stuffed up my life. You had no right to do what you did to me. Also making me do those things that you wanted me to do to you over and over again. I also felt that you did not have the right to bash me the way you did. You have destroyed my life once again just because you could not have your own way.

Now I will tell you what I am going through. I feel that I am going through hell because of what you have done to me. I feel that of all the times you have forced me to have sex with you this time was the worst to cope with because my husband was not around. I felt that when my husband was around I would be ok but now that he isn't around I feel that you still have a hold on me and you will have a hold on me for the rest of my life. I am afraid of what is going to happen.

You have asked me to forgive you for what you have done to me. I will never forgive you. You can rot in hell before I forgive you. You have also told me that you changed but you have not shown me that you have changed. Deep down I know that you will never change. You also used your children to try to change my mind about you. Also you tried to use mother to change my mind as well by telling me that she was ashamed of the way I turned out. You said that is why mother would not tell me that she was dying until it was too late

In a way it was my fault for what I am going though. If I did not let you in that day I would not be in the mess that I am in now. I would not feel the way I am feeling. Also I am feeling so much guilt about what I have done. I think that my husband would be ashamed of what I have done also. One day I hope that my husband would forgive me for what I have done in my life.

Now I will tell you how I really feel about you. You are a bloody bastard for what you have done to me over the years. Also what you have done to me since my husband died. One day you will have to pay for what you have done. I hope you rot in hell and you never hurt me again.

Your sister Elly

To my brother Jack

I am writing this to you because I felt that I should do this. I would like to tell you what I been going though since I have been remembering things from my past.

First I would like to say that you have destroyed my life once again. You had no right to do what you did to me. You had no right making me pregnant and forcing me to have an Abortion. You did this so no one would know what you were doing to me. I was only 13 years old I was still a child. I am feeling that you should have not done what you did to me. It should have been someone that I loved not my brother who I hate so much.

You have destroyed my life and the dreams that I had. I dreamed what every little girl dreams about. In my life I only wanted to be happy. I wanted to do two things in my life to get married and have children. My dreams were destroyed. If it was not for you I would have been happy. I might have had a family that I could have loved? All I wanted was to have a normal life.

Only a few weeks you made me have sex with your mates. You also made them pay you to have sex with me. I felt like a prostitute and a slut. Now I know what you meant when you said that mother would be ashamed of me. I know that she would have been now that I know what I have done.

Until I do something about you I feel that I am living in hell. I am hoping it will stop one day before it is too late for me. I really hope that I will be happy again.

Your sister Elly

To my brother Jack

I am writing this to you because I feel that I should write this letter to you. I am going to tell you how I feel about you and what you have done to my life.

You have destroyed my life by having sex with me and also making me do what you wanted me do to you while you were having sex. I still can't understand why you did this to me I was your little sister who you should have loved like a big brother. To me sex should have been a beautiful thing not the ugly word that you made it.

I was only ten years old when you started to take over my life by taking a special part of me, which was my childhood. You knew it was not right for you to have sex with me. Also to make me do what you wanted me to do to you. You had the power over me because you found out information about personal things. You used that against me to get me to do whatever you wanted. I was scared to not do what you told me to do. I did not want you to tell anyone about these secrets. You made me feel dirty, hurt, ashamed, cheap and guilty. I should not have done anything; I should have told someone.

Do you know why I went to live with the person that I ended up marrying? It was not because I loved him. It was to get away from you. You still had a hold on me. You still wanted me to do the things that you told me to do when I was growing up. When he asked me to marry him I was not in love with him but I saw an easy way out. I did finally fell in love with him a few months after.

You also stuffed my life up with my husband. You were the cause of the trouble I was having. My husband could not understand why I did not give him sex when he wanted it. I told him NO most of the time. I knew it was not fair on him. He blamed himself; he would say it was because of his diabetes. I was not going to tell him the truth.

When you came to stay with us I did not want to believe that you wanted me again. But when my husband had to go out for those few hours that day I knew what you wanted. I was afraid to stop you. When you took me back to my childhood I felt like that small defenceless child again. You know how to get to me, don't you?

After that day I felt guilty about what I had done. I could not live the way I was I started to have nightmares every night. The nightmares were getting worse to cope with. I could not live in hell any longer so when my husband asked me about the nightmares I had to tell him what you had made me do. It made us argue. A few days later my husband died.

Now I will tell you how I feel about you. You are a Bastard for what you have made me do to you. The things I had to do to you have made me ill. I will never forgive you for what you have put me through. I hate you and I wish you were DEAD. I hope one day soon it will become true. Then I can be happy again.

Your sister Elly

Four

LIFE WITH MY HUSBAND

I first met Peter when I was about 4-5 years old. He would have been 25 years old and was married. My mother knew his mother quite well. They would have morning tea together, taking turns making scones, cake and biscuits. The Thompson and Martin families associated together regularly. Peter would play around and tickle me to make me laugh. I could not have realised how our lives eventually would come together.

Rosemary, my oldest sister, was hanging around with Peter's brother Richard and eventually they decided to move in together. Mother didn't want her to but she had no choice in the matter. She thought if she tried to stop Rosemary from going she would lose her for good. She couldn't take that; her daughter going off with a man almost twice her age and a divorced man with children, at that. What could she do? My sister was sixteen, legally old enough to go with Richard.

Many years later, aged 22, I again saw Peter at my sister's place. We started talking about stuff we had been doing. He told me that his wife had left him after twenty years of marriage. She had gone off with his best friend. Actually, Peter had had his suspicions that something was going on. So one day, he went home for lunch but decided he would come in through the back way. He caught the two of them in bed. His wife didn't hang around much longer.

Peter had six grown children, three boys and three girls, ranging in age from 12 to 22. The oldest, Dianne, was the same age as me! Peter was looking for someone to come and help him out for six weeks while the grape-picking season was on; he lived in the southeast of the state where there is a major wine industry. He knew he would be working up to eighteen hours a day and then have to come home and do everything for his children. He was looking for someone to make sure his children were up for school and to cook for them.

I told him I would help him out if he wanted me to and he was grateful for this offer. So we arranged that I would come and help out for the next six weeks. Now I had to tell Mum that I was going to do this. As expected, she was not happy about my going to stay with Peter. Despite the friendship between our two families, Peter was, after all, a divorced man and I was her youngest daughter, the baby of the family. And I had just moved into my own flat about six weeks before. I had decided that I needed to prove to my mum I could take care of myself. So she was feeling very protective.

When Jack heard that I was going, he went crazy. He realised he would not be in control of me while I was not with him. So he came around with two of my brothers and my former best girlfriend to try to persuade me not to go. It didn't change my mind at all. Instead, it just made me more determined to go.

But, as usual, Jack wasn't going to take "no" for an answer. The next day, when the car was packed up ready to go, the local police arrived at my flat. They said they had received information that Peter and I had drugs and were taking them with us to sell. I was in shock – why was this happening to me? I started to imagine myself being arrested, going to court, and winding up in jail. The police searched Peter's car and all my stuff, but found nothing. The constable then asked if we had had an argument with anyone. We told him about the incident with Jack the night before. Hearing this, the police left and we set off for Peter's place.

I had offered to go to Peter's because it would be an opportunity to escape from Jack. I knew that if I didn't somehow get away, my brother would continue to abuse me. Living in my own flat had shown that I could take care of myself. But I did not see it as a long-term arrangement. Going to Peter's seemed like an ideal way to be out of Jack's reach. I knew my brother wouldn't come to Peter's place, as he would not be in control anymore.

When I arrived at Peter's, things were very tense, particularly between the children and me. I didn't know what I was getting into and they didn't want me there. It showed on their faces and in their secretive, conspiring whispers. They thought that I would be trying to take over from their mother. That certainly was not my intention, as I planned to be there for only six weeks. As it turned out, six weeks became twenty-one years.

Peter's children did everything they could to get rid of me. I suspect they had had a meeting among themselves before I arrived to devise ways for making me leave. The older kids would get Dennis, the youngest, to do all the dirty work. My bed seemed to be a favourite target. One night, I pulled back the covers to find liquid detergent spread in the middle of the mattress. I think the kids thought they were going to be in big trouble, and that I would tell their father. But I didn't and just changed the bed with sheets I had brought from home and washed the dirty linen in the morning.

But the attacks on my bed continued. Not long after, following a busy day and feeling pretty stuffed, I discovered a large frog hiding under the sheets. Dennis had been at it again. In those early weeks, I was called names, sworn at, had things thrown at me, and was reminded that I was not their mother and that they did not want me there. Not doing chores and wagging school were also part of the plan. Of course, none of these things were done in front of their father, who would often take their side anyway if I brought their behaviour to his attention.

Turns out the Martin children were well-known in the community for their mischievous ways. They weren't really "bad" but they liked to test the boundaries and push people's buttons to see how far they could get. So they had a bit of a reputation. Dennis, for example, had been given a trail bike for his 13th birthday. Peter told him to only ride the bike among the grapevines. But, when Peter was at work, Dennis decided to skip school and go into town to see his girlfriend. With his father's warning in mind, Dennis drove through the grapevines, then across a side road, through more vines, across another road, more vines, more roads - until he arrived in town.

When school was due to come out, Dennis finished his visit in order to arrive home when the school bus got there. To get back in time, he needed to take the roads all the way. Unfortunately for Dennis, the police spotted him. With his knowledge of the grapevines, Dennis tried to get away by cutting through the vineyards. But the police already had identified Dennis and headed for the house, pulling in the drive just after Peter arrived from work. Another episode involving the Martin family entered the police records.

It seemed to run in the family. Not long after, Peter's oldest son Wayne, who had been living for some time in Western Australia, came home for a visit. Having driven all the way from WA, he perhaps was eager to finish his trip. For he was detected travelling at 160 kph through several towns on the way to his father's house. Eventually, he stopped for petrol and the police caught up with him. They questioned Wayne and asked him to identify himself. Upon hearing who he was, the attending officer exclaimed, "Oh no, not another bloody Martin!"

Peter also was drinking and this made my situation worse. The first thing he would do after he got home was to get a beer out of the fridge. If there was no beer he would drink red wine or sherry in a 4-litre flagon. At that time wine and beer were cheap. Peter was an alcoholic but would not admit it.

He used to drink every night when he came home from work. He would fall off to sleep in his chair then wake up and go to bed. His children would encourage him to drink more because they could get anything they wanted while he was drunk. On the weekends Peter and his drinking mate would meet up around 8:00am with booze and go into the shed or the driveway and drink all day. When they finished off what they were drinking, they would drive to the bottle shop in the nearest town to get more, taking the back roads to avoid being caught by the local police. Peter would not eat when he was drinking with his mate. I would cook his meal but then would have to put it in the fridge until he was ready to eat. It could be the early hours of the morning before he did.

Peter used to bash me up when he was drinking; he had to be drunk for him to do it. Not all the time but sometimes. The first time he hit me was in front of his children. It was because I would not allow Dennis to borrow my radio to have in his room. Peter was angry with me because I had said no. He started to throw punches at me, repeatedly hitting me around the face and neck. The next morning I was all bruised around the neck. This should have made me go back to Mum's. But I didn't because I didn't want her to find out what had happened. And my brother would have that control again. I could not go through that so I stayed with Peter.

After Peter's children saw their father hitting me, his second oldest son thought he would try it too. He did it while his father was out so he wouldn't get into trouble. He would tell his father I had fallen over and hurt myself. I tried to tell Peter the truth but he believed his son. I felt caught between a rock and a hard place, between getting bashed at Peter's or being abused by my brother. I felt it was better to be bashed than to be abused again, so that's why I stayed. I didn't want to go back to my brother being in control.

My six-week stay with Peter turned into months, then longer. After about four months, Peter asked me to marry him. I thought about it for a while. I didn't love him at that time but I thought getting married would be good for me. All I was thinking about was that my brother would not have the control over me if I married Peter. That was the reason I said yes. Peter didn't know the real reason.

We got married as soon as Peter's divorce came though, roughly one year after my arrival at Peter's. Peter was a Catholic and in those days, being divorced, you were not allowed to re-marry in the church. We decided to be married in the courthouse in Adelaide. We had only two other people there – Peter's drinking mate and his wife, who were our witnesses. Peter's children weren't present - they didn't want anything to do with our marriage. From day one, they "hated my guts" and Peter knew this. In fact, he announced our wedding plans by saying, "I'm going to marry Elly whether you like it or not!" Not the greatest way to start married life.

However, Peter really wanted us to be married. He did not want to be lonely for the rest of his life. In fact, he had wanted to marry me years before. He was in love with me when I was a teenager but I was too young to marry. He told a friend that one day he would be married to me. And it came true. That friend told me about this in later years, after Peter had died.

After we were married, we went to a local hotel and had dinner and a few drinks. My new husband and his mate got drunk and his wife had to drive us all home.

Now that we were married, Peter demanded sex whenever he wanted it, whether I did or not. We used to fight about this all the time. Peter was like my brother. He would force me into saying yes to sex. This took me back to my childhood when my brother had forced me into having sex with him. I was that little girl again - trapped, trapped, trapped. When he had been drinking, Peter used to say he married me to have sex whenever he wanted, as I was his wife, his possession.

When he was not drinking, Peter was a different person. He was a caring, loving husband. He would not argue and he would do jobs around the house. He would make me breakfast in bed on Sunday mornings. He would cook a BBQ with steak, sausages, potatoes, and onions and sometimes cook fish in foil. He was a good father to his children. He went without to give to his children. He made sure we had food and all the bills were paid before he started to drink, before he got to the booze. Peter was a good person in his own way. I know that he never meant to hurt me the way he did.

My husband always had the power and control with sex and bills and how much he would drink. When he wanted to go and see his parents and brother, he always said that I had to go whether I wanted to or not. So very early every Sunday morning, at 6.00am, we would go down to see Peter's family for a couple of hours then come back and have breakfast. I hated going there so much that I was ill in my stomach before I left home. When we arrived I would start to shake inside and out because I had to go into their house. I hated going there because Peter's brother was Richard, the one who abused me when I went to visit my sister Rosemary. When Peter was out of the room, Richard would talk about "stuff". He bought things at sex shops and showed them to me to try to get me sexually interested. This happened nearly every time we went to their house. Of course, I never responded to these approaches but I knew I would have to face them each time. Richard was a very different person to Peter.

We each had our own roles in the house and I had to get up when Peter did. I did the housework like dishes, making the bed, washing, ironing, vacuuming and washing the floors. My husband would be the one for the outdoor chores like the lawns, cleaning up after the dogs, sweeping the paths, and washing the cars and truck.

When I first went to stay with Peter, our relationship was troubled and scary. This was because I didn't want Peter to have any reason to send me back to Adelaide. I knew if I went back there my brother would have that power and control over me once again. Peter and I were caring for each other - I was looking after an alcoholic with diabetes and he was looking after me with my cerebral palsy.

Sometimes I felt abused with my husband because of the bashings he gave me over this time. I took it because I didn't have anywhere else to go. Also I didn't know any different. I had been abused most of my life and that's the way I was brought up with all the men in my life.

At the same time, I felt safe with my husband knowing that my brother would not come to our place and cause a scene. My brother knew if he turned up that Peter would do some serious damage to him for calling the police on us the day that I left with Peter.

Peter and I both had hidden reasons for this marriage. My husband's was because of what his first wife did to him. She left him in debt. She took nearly everything in the house while Peter was at work and cleared out the money in their accounts in the bank. She left him with $2.00 in his pocket. The children had very few clothes. That's why Peter wanted me to be there, to help him out. He was hoping I would not be like his first wife.

I did finally fall in love with Peter. It was not with the alcoholic that I first saw but with the other person that he showed me over time. The one who could be caring, loving, gentle and kind.

I gained a lot from being married to Peter. I could finally be happy in a relationship that I never had before. I became stronger within myself. Ironically, it was Peter's constant drinking that made me stronger. I knew that whatever I needed, I had to do for myself – or else go insane with everything that was wrong in my life.

There are some events that were particularly special and memorable during my time with Peter. We went to Gellibrand in the rain forests of southwest Victoria, to a house owned by a couple we knew. We tried to go there nearly every year, for a couple of weeks to get away from home. It was nice there because there was no shop for miles, no phone to worry about, and no TV. It was good just us two spending the time together - without the hassle of the children. We used to go away camping on the weekends. We'd leave Friday after work until Sunday late in the afternoon. It was good to make a fire for the billy tea and toast and to cook eggs and bacon. It was a different taste than what you cook at home.

In 1983, major bushfires hit South Australia, the Ash Wednesday fires. We could see and smell the fires from where we lived. After the fire was controlled they were asking people to help with the clean up. Where Peter worked they asked about trucks and forklifts and manpower. Peter was one who was asked by his boss to help and there was another man that Peter took with him. When they reached the bushfire area, Peter and the other men saw things they had never seen before. There were burnt cattle and sheep that had tried to go somewhere safe. The dead cattle were blown up with blowflies and had bloated stomachs. Peter and the others worked there all week.

Peter was really affected by this experience. He had had to see lots of animals dead and disfigured. When the men tried to clear up the carcasses with forklifts, they had to be careful or the bodies would fall apart or burst. From seeing all this, Peter was not able to eat the meals I prepared for him, particularly if they involved meat. But there was one good thing. A baby calf had survived the fires and Peter brought the calf home. We decided to keep it and we raised it for the next 18 months.

Peter liked rabbit trapping – this was when you could set traps legally. He had both traps and ferrets, which were used to chase the rabbits out of their holes. We used to stay out overnight in the hills and Peter would set all the traps near the rabbit holes by dusk. He would then wake up early to check the traps and see if he had caught anything. If there were rabbits in the traps, he would skin and clean them and put them into an esky to bring back home. When we arrived home I would freeze some of them. The rest I would make into rabbit stew, roast rabbit, boiled and fried rabbit - but best of all was the curried rabbit that I made. Peter always said never buy a rabbit from the butchers, as you don't know how long they have had them in the shop. Fresh is the best.

Other times we went fishing at Robe in the southeast. My husband and his youngest son, Dennis, and I would go. Peter would have to bait my fishing line, as I didn't want to touch the worms to put onto the hook. Dennis would want to bet with me who would catch the first fish. Peter used to laugh at us when we bet on stuff as I mostly won every time.

We would go shopping and Peter would get us a treat; we would get a packet of Wagon Wheels or cream buns. With the Wagon Wheels there were 6 in the packet, which meant we could have 3 each. Peter only had one when his blood sugar was down to the right level. He would know if I took an extra Wagon Wheel – even though I always denied this! We also would buy a 4-litre ice cream and Peter would say, after he took his blood level and if it was low, he could have a bowl of ice cream tonight.

Peter and I drank a lot of coffee and tea after he gave up the booze. We would have up to 30 cups a day, some times more. It depended on the day. Peter had a saying - if he wanted a second cup of tea, it was "it's a dry argument", which meant to put the kettle on and have another cuppa. We liked to drink from mugs and Peter had seen these big mugs while we were shopping; he got one for each of us. These mugs were very high and would hold about one and a half cups in them.

My husband loved roses so he planted them around the back garden and in the front yard. He used to go out every morning and evening to feel the roses and see if they are ready to drop onto the ground. He would check each rose to see if it was ready to open. If they were ready he would sometimes pick them to bring into the house. He would pick a rose before it fell to the ground because he thought they were most beautiful while on their stems.

Another thing that Peter loved was his cars. It was not unusual for Peter to have three or four vehicles at one time. Over the years, I saw many cars, trucks and motorcycles sitting in our driveway. Peter would see something for sale cheap, and he'd buy it. Usually, he would check with me before buying. But even if I said "No!" he would still go ahead. His excuse was that he had bought it with his own money. Once, while I was in New Zealand visiting my good friend Robyn, who had been my nurse at Somerton, Peter rang. I was surprised to hear from him because he wouldn't normally call when I was away. However, he wanted to warn me that he had bought another truck. He knew that I would have gone mad when I got home and saw this new vehicle sitting there. He wanted me to have time to calm down before I flew back. There was method in his madness. He knew that I couldn't yell at him over the phone, in front of Robyn. I just had to accept that the deed was done.

Peter told me never to do two things while I was married to him - (a) don't cut your long hair and (b) don't start smoking. He loved my long hair and used to run his fingers through it. My hair was thick, that's why. About smoking, he told me if I started he would divorce me. One day we were having a disagreement about something. I decided to go to the shop and get a packet of smokes. I came back and lit up a cigarette in front of Peter. I had one puff and nearly choked! I have never done it again. I wanted to see if he would divorce me because of smoking - he never did!

Peter and his drinking mate started a vegetable garden on a ½ acre of land they rented. They planted a lot of vegetables to sell to the shops. Unfortunately, they would use their profits to buy more booze. They grew a veritable "cornucopia" of produce - pumpkins, peas, beans, zucchini, carrots, silver beet, cucumber, watermelon, rockmelon, potatoes, cauliflower, cabbage, capsicums, zucchini and onions. We had plenty for us to freeze and have fresh every day. I remember when Peter came home with the peas we would eat more than we would shell. He was getting tired of us doing this, so one day he shut himself in the bedroom and shelled them all himself. He even blanched them himself too.

As a result of drinking and smoking for over 40 years, Peter developed diabetes. When he found out about his diabetes, he had already had it for 4 years. The doctor put Peter on diabetic tablets, then after a while he was put on insulin. It was too late by then. He still drank a lot. His diabetes forced him to give up his job as he became blind in one eye. We then had to move to Adelaide for treatment. He had to have 14 laser treatments on his blind eye. His sight returned but he was colour blind. One morning, Peter woke me up in the early hours to give me some surprising news - he was going to give up the drink and smokes. But it was too late when he did. As his diabetes got worse, Peter worried about me as I was having health problems at the same time. He told me that he didn't want me to have an operation on any part of my back, as he was worried I was going to be in a wheelchair for the rest of my life. Meanwhile, Peter had heart problems that were getting worse – but he didn't tell me.

When he gave up the booze and the smokes he changed for the better. We would laugh together and even cried together. We did new things together; we'd go on long drives for a day trip somewhere nice. Peter even started to tell me he loved me. When he was drinking, he would never say these words. He started to be on my side when his children said things about me. He realized that things with the children were not my fault.

One conversation we often had was about whether it would be better to have a female Prime Minister to run Australia. I told Peter that a female Prime Minister might be better than all the males we'd already had. Peter was sceptical and said it would never happen in his lifetime. To stir things up between us, he said that he particularly wouldn't want me as Prime Minister.

He predicted I would help everyone that needed a hand out and that wouldn't be good for the government. I said, if I was Prime Minister, there wouldn't be problems like there are with the health system, there would be more support and resources for pensioners, there'd be better education, and there wouldn't be poor people any more, everyone would be on the same level. In one way, Peter was right. Australia did get a female Prime Minister – but it didn't happen in his lifetime.

I remember on my 34th birthday he wanted to give me a party because I had never celebrated one before. So he arranged with our friends to help him do the party. He got them to help him with the food and he gave them money to get the things he wanted them to make. One person brought roast chicken, roast potatoes, glazed carrots. Another one brought the chicken curry and stir-fry. Another person made coleslaw, pasta, potato, seafood salads and cold meats. Another couple of friends made desserts - pavlova, lemon meringue, brandy snaps, apple pie and fruit in jelly.

Peter told me that he wanted to make a big pot of curried sausages to put into the freezer but that was not the real reason. He knew that I would not question it as we did this often - making stuff for the freezer.

When everyone came over on Saturday I was so surprised because my husband did something for me that no one else had ever done before. I was so glad that he made it possible – and without my help!

For my 40th birthday, I had a bigger party. This time, I had someone make everything without imposing on friends. The venue was at the rear of a good friend's place in a big room. It had a kitchen in the room where we could warm things up and serve them. I had my aunt and uncle there for that night. It was the first time ever I had any of my family there with me. It was my aunt from my mother's side of the family. My uncle said a speech on my behalf about my life. It was good that they were there. I will have that memory for the rest of my life and the photos I have of them.

When Peter turned 60, I gave him a party, a BBQ with friends in the back yard. Some of his children came with their partners and children. To make him happy I had to ask them. His children kept to themselves drinking while I mixed with our friends. My husband was helping with the cooking. We had a lot of food there for everyone.

After our friends had left arguments arose between his children and me about why the other children were not invited. Peter finally had enough and told his daughter's partner to leave because he had insulted me. I felt proud that Peter put me before his family.

Peter and I were married for almost 21 years. During that time, we never had any children. When I was eighteen years old, I had my tubes done because I thought I didn't want to have a child with a disability and I didn't think that I would ever get married. I never told anyone about this. When I got married, I tried to have my tubes reversed so I could give a child to Peter. But due to the way they had operated, it could not be reversed. Ironically when I was in hospital to get my tubes reversed, I was in a ward with three women who were having abortions. I was angry with them for getting pregnant and because they were trying to kill their unborn children. While I was trying to achieve a pregnancy, they were seeking to abort theirs

Top left: Flatbed truck for moving picking machines

Above, left: Grape picking machine

Bottom: Grape picking

Wine vineyards, South Australia

Wine vineyards, South Australia

Five

DEATHS

Death has played a big part in my life. Over the years, I have lost all of the people who have meant the most to me. It started when my mother died.

Mum was nearly 62 when she lost her battle with cancer. It was 11 days before my 28th birthday. My family had kept her illness away from me for a long time – I still don't know exactly how long Mum had been sick. Only my dad and my sister Helen, with whom Dad was living, knew how bad she was. The rest of the family didn't know the seriousness of the illness. When I was finally told, it was only four days before Mum died.

Peter and I had just moved from McLaren Vale to a place up north. We'd been at the caravan park less than a month when

Helen came by and said, "If you want to see Mum, you'd better come to my place tomorrow morning." All I knew at that point was that Helen was bringing Mum home to her and Dad's house for a weekend visit. Only later did I find out that my sister had confided in Peter that I would need him more than ever. I had no inkling of what I was to experience the next day.

When Peter and I arrived at Helen's, we knocked and my sister called out to come in. Two of my brothers were already there and everyone was sitting at the kitchen table. Peter went in first, then me. Then I saw my mum - and I could not speak. I was in shock. She weighed only six stone; she had no hair. She was slumped over in her chair, so weak she couldn't lift her head to look at anyone. Neither could she talk because the cancer had affected her voice.

It was too much to face. Crying, I left the kitchen and went outside to where our car was parked. Why had no one warned me what to expect or how Mum would look? Peter and Helen followed me out. I was angry with everyone for not telling me what was going on. I asked my sister why she hadn't warned me. Helen said that she hadn't known how to tell me about Mum. And she said that Dad didn't want me to know how sick Mum was. They didn't want me to worry or get stressed. They knew how much I loved Mum and that I would do anything for her. And they said they were concerned for my own health. I hated my sister and Dad for not telling before that day but I understood why they concealed it from me.

After a while, I regained some composure. I went back inside and put on a brave front for Mum but this was difficult. All I was thinking was "How could God do this to my mother?" She didn't deserve to die like this. Mum was a good person. I was shocked at her appearance and condition. I couldn't even hug her or talk with her. I looked around at all my family and they saw how distressed I was. Dad knew I was upset and prevented me from getting into a discussion about why I hadn't been told.

During the day, Mum got worse so Dad and Helen decided to take her to the Royal Adelaide Hospital. Dad announced that the only people who could go with Mum were my sister and my two brothers. I couldn't believe what I was hearing. Again, I was being kept out. I told Dad I had the right to be there and made a fuss about not going with them. Dad relented. But he told Helen she was the only person allowed in the room with mother at the hospital.

After my three siblings and I admitted Mum to the hospital, we returned home. Overnight she deteriorated and was transferred to the Intensive Care Unit. She was put on machines to help her live a little longer. On Saturday Dad and Helen went to see her and thought it was time to tell the family to come to the hospital. Peter and I went down but when we got there, Dad wouldn't allow us to see her. Because he was still married to her, he wanted to be the one who was with her if and when she died.

In the midst of all this activity and upset, Peter and I had an interview about a farmhouse to rent. We needed to move out of our temporary accommodation at the caravan park almost straight away. So Monday morning we drove to the nearest town to buy some furniture for the house. While there, I called my sister from a phone box. She told me that I needed to come to her house. I asked if it was Mother. Helen answered, "Yes."

At Helen's, she told me that Mum was worse and did not have long to live. We knew we had to go to the hospital. In the waiting room outside intensive care, a nurse spoke to Dad. Apparently it was not looking good and Mum had only hours. Dad was again making all the decisions about who could see her. First it was Dad and my sister, and then my two brothers went in. When my dad came out to the waiting room again I told him I wanted to see Mother. He tried to stop me again. We had a few words and I told him he wasn't going to prevent me from seeing her. Peter stood up for me too.

After a few minutes Helen came out and then accompanied me in. It was terrible to see Mum lying there surrounded by machines. She wasn't in pain any more – she looked peaceful. There were tubes and things all around and the nurses were busy checking the machines and tending to her. I just stood in silence. After about 15 minutes, I told Helen I was leaving. That was the last time I saw Mother.

Soon after, a doctor came and said Mum had very little time left. Dad and Helen went in. They were the only ones there when she died. I just sat with Peter and my brothers. I didn't want to see her again, didn't want to see her dead. It wasn't long before Dad came out and said she was gone. I looked at Peter and I couldn't cry at all.

After a while we went back to Dad and Helen's place, with the rest of my brothers and sisters. I just wanted to be alone but my sister wouldn't allow that. She kept watching me like a hawk. Eventually Dad told Helen to ring and make arrangements for Mother's funeral. Once these arrangements were completed, we had to write something for the newspaper about Mother. I decided I would do this. I found it hard to express how I felt about my mother, to write it in the way I wanted to say it. I felt I had to say something from my heart that expressed all my feelings about Mum and her death - my love, heartbreak, sorrow, and pain. This was the first time I'd had to write about a death. As I put down the words about her passing, memories surfaced, causing me to break down and cry. It was one of the hardest things I have ever done.

It was four years after my mother died that I again experienced death. My sister Helen ended her own life. She was thirty-eight years old.

After my mother's death Helen started to feel so much guilt about what was happening between Dad and her. They were living like a married couple instead of how a father and a daughter should. So that no one would figure out what was going on, they made up a bedroom for my sister with two beds so if anyone stayed there were no questions. There was another room for the children when they returned home for the weekends. During the week they attended a special school due to their disabilities.

Mother had kept the family together while she was alive. Whenever anyone in the family was in trouble, Mum was there to help. She had helped Helen with the children and provided money, clothes and food when needed. But she never talked about what was happening between my dad and my sister.

After Mum's death, Helen couldn't cope. She did things that would have angered Mum if she were still alive.

Helen started going out to hotels nearly every night drinking. She'd try to come home late when she thought Dad was in bed for the night. But sometimes he was still up waiting up for her. Dad tried to stop her drinking but she took no notice of him. He started hitting my sister to try to stop her. He had never hit her before this. He knew that he had lost control over Helen.

My sister decided the only way out of this situation was to end her own life. She started going to different doctors around the city, suburbs and country area. She went back to the doctors who gave her what she wanted. She told them she could not sleep and she convinced them to give her sleeping pills. My sister even asked me about the GP I was seeing. She asked me to get her some tablets, but I refused.

Then she started to mix the booze and sleeping tablets together. There were times when she called in to my house after a few drinks. Peter and I now lived closer to the city, about 100 kilometres from my dad and Helen. It normally would take over an hour to drive this distance. When she had been drinking, Helen sometimes made it within half an hour. She could hide how much she was drinking and she was also taking risks.

Helen was worried about her children should anything happened to her. She asked me if I'd look after them if she wasn't around. My sister didn't want any of my brothers to have the children. She was worried that my brothers would take control of the children in order to get their disability pensions. She knew I would not do any such thing. I told her that I would make sure that my brothers didn't do anything to the children. She was happy that I agreed to this.

My sister waited until her children were old enough to be more independent before she suicided. I didn't know that she was thinking about suicide when she asked me about her children. Peter and I had told her she would be around for a long time. But Helen had often told me she was not going to be around after forty.

At times my sister rang Lifeline to talk to someone. They would try to keep her on the phone as long as they could. Sometimes she would simply hang up.

Just before her suicide, Helen and Dad visited me. She was worried about me as I was having trouble with a few things in my life at that time. She knew that I had sleeping tablets. My sister had told Dad that she thought I would take them and do something to myself. That's why they came over that night. My sister wanted the tablets for herself because her doctors wouldn't prescribe any more. So she took my new bottle of tablets from my bedroom drawer without my knowledge.

The night my sister ended her life she didn't even ring Lifeline. She drank a lot, took a whole bottle of tablets, and went to bed. Dad found her dead in her bed the next day.

I felt guilty about of my sister's death and this is why I haven't kept or taken any more sleeping tablets to this day. I feel that if those sleeping tablets hadn't been in the house that night my sister might still be alive.

Because their house had been a Housing Trust home in Helen's name, my dad could not stay there. He had to go into a nursing home after her death. He had a room all to himself, with a bed, a dressing table and a wardrobe. There was a communal dining area and television room. Dad had to pay a lot to go into the nursing home. He had to give them most of his pension. He had a little money left to buy toiletries and smokes.

Very few people went to visit him. My brothers and my other sister didn't want anything to do with him after my sister died. That's when I decided that I had to go to see him once a week. Even though I hated him, I felt obligated to visit him. He was still my dad. Peter was not sure this was a good thing but he took me anyway.

Dad loved chocolate but he couldn't buy any, so every time I visited I brought him some. Then I decided to make homemade chocolate for him. I bought some dark and white chocolate buttons, and some chocolate moulds with different designs. I made some plain dark chocolate ones and white chocolates. I then mixed the chocolate and made half dark and half white chocolates. You might wonder why I bothered, why I did anything for him. He was still my father, regardless of how I felt about him.

Sometimes we took Dad for a drive to help him get over losing my sister but it never helped much. We'd go for a counter meal at a hotel for lunch and he'd have a beer sometimes. We'd always have him back to the nursing home around 3:00pm.

Eleven months after my sister's death Dad had a heart attack during the night and died. The staff found him in the morning and because my eldest sister Rosemary was the next of kin she was told first. Rosemary rang all of us and made arrangements to meet at the nursing home to decide about his funeral. We knew he was going to be buried with Mum, as they never got a divorce.

Rosemary wanted us all to put money toward Dad's funeral. Some of my brothers didn't want to, so only two brothers, my sister and I helped with his funeral. Then Rosemary found out that Dad had been saving to put a headstone on Helen's grave. Rosemary wanted that money to go toward the funeral. I made a fuss about this, as I knew that Dad wanted that money to go towards Helen's stone. He had been saving up for that ever since she died. He wanted to do it for my sister and her children. In the end, I got my way. My sister's stone was paid for with Dad's money, and four of us split the cost of his funeral.

Eight months after my dad's death, my oldest brother Michael drowned. Michael was the one who'd done lots of fun things with me when I was young. This was the third death in 18 months.

Michael suffered with diabetes and Parkinson's disease. When Mum died Michael had to find another place to live, as he could not look after himself because his diabetes and Parkinson's were getting worse. The shaking associated with Parkinson's affected his whole body, he could only walk with short shuffling steps, and he eventually lost his voice. He wound up moving from hostel to hostel, staying a few months at each. Michael constantly wet himself, and because of this, none of my family wanted him to live with them.

Michael asked me if I would be his next to kin if anything happened to him. What else could I say but yes. Peter didn't think it was a good idea about being next to kin but he knew what it meant to me.

The day my brother drowned he had gone to the beach. It was very hot that day. He couldn't swim at all and was scared of the water. I can remember going down to Glenelg when we were young, where the showgrounds were, and Michael would never go near the water. Even when he took a bath, he didn't fill the tub very much! I can't understand why he went near the water that day.

Michael's body was found floating near the shore at about 2.00pm. The police didn't know if a murder had been committed or if it was suicide. That evening, after the police had determined who Michael was, probably from his pension card, they came to inform me of his death. But I wasn't home that night – I had gone to visit a Filipino friend just around the corner, and she and her mother were trying to teach me a Filipino card game. When Peter came to my friend's house and told me about Michael, I was shocked - I didn't know what to say. When we got home, I had to ring the rest of the family with the news.

Being next to kin I had to identify his body. The next day another of my brothers and I met a constable. We were taken into a small room and a trolley was wheeled out on the other side of a glass window. When I saw the male adult body lying there, with only the face showing, I immediately recognised it as Michael. But his face looked as if it was twice its normal size, because of him being in the water. I actually screamed. This was the first time I had seen a dead body. When my other family members died, they were placed in caskets and I didn't see them.

I knew my brother well and he would never have taken his own life after what Helen had done. After Helen suicided, Michael said that someone who took their own life was stupid and he would never do that. And I believed him. He was on a lot of medication for his illnesses and if he had wanted to kill himself he could have taken all his tablets. And he certainly wouldn't have wanted to die in the water. The coroner reported the cause of death as "salt water drowning". While I don't know for sure, I believe that Michael fell, couldn't get up, and the tide came in while he was unconscious.

Five years later another one of my brothers, Paul, died at the age of 49 from lung cancer. Paul was ten years older than me and was a smoker nearly all his life. When he died I didn't learn about it until several months later. The rest ofthe family never told me. The reason they gave me was that no one knew where I was living at that time. In reality, I had been living at my place for a few years before Paul died and my oldest sister knew where I was. So I didn't get to go to his funeral and I didn't know how or where he was buried until it was too late to say anything. Wayne, the brother he was living with, gave him a "pauper's funeral". Paul always had money and would have had enough to pay for his own funeral. But Wayne had different ideas. I think Wayne saw this as a chance to get Paul's money, and he somehow got the State to pay for the burial. So Paul is buried in an unmarked grave; he deserved more than this. I have visited his grave only once and will not go back again. It was too upsetting to see how he had been treated by my family. I am determined that one day I will save enough money to pay for a proper funeral for him.

Death again entered my life four years later. My husband Peter was only 61 years old; I was only 42. That was too young for him to leave me. He died because of his diabetes.

Peter never really took his diabetes seriously – until it was too late. He drank too much and smoked 20-25 of his own-rolled cigarettes every day. One morning at home he had a small heart attack and was taken to hospital by ambulance. After Peter was admitted, I stayed with him until late afternoon. When I told the nurse I needed to go home for a while; she said Peter would be okay until I returned. So I went home, had a shower, got something to eat, and fed the animals. When I rang the hospital a few hours later, they said there was no change and I told them I'd come back the next morning.

But I never saw Peter alive again. Soon after I woke the next day, I received a call to come as soon as possible. I rang a friend to drive me, and contacted Peter's daughter while I waited. She didn't seem to care about me, didn't ask if I wanted a ride. When I got there, it was 20 minutes too late. Peter had died of a major heart attack.

The curtains were drawn around Peter's bed. When I went through the curtains, I found Peter's daughter and her boyfriend sitting next to his bed, and some other people I didn't even know. They were probably some relatives of Peter – I never got to know much about his family. Peter was lying there. I was in shock; no one would talk to me. I should have been the first person to see Peter. It was a horrible experience.

Soon Peter's oldest son arrived. He looked at his father, and then turned to me. My husband was not even cold when his son asked, "Did Dad have a will?" I said I had a copy at home.

They all came back to my place and read the will. Everything had been left to me. My husband knew if he didn't make a will, his children would take everything. Their father was not dead for an hour and a half when this happened.

Once they knew that they wouldn't be getting anything, Peter's children were not happy. They complained about how it was unfair. They didn't help me with any of the costs for Peter's burial and I wound up paying for his funeral and headstone on my own. I was happy to do this, but it was very hard to do everything. I had my own bills, plus Peter's to pay. It took me a long time and I had to do without a lot of things to make the payments. But I did it all myself.

Things didn't get any better. At Peter's funeral his children and relations sat on one side of the chapel, and I and my friends on the other side. They didn't come up and talk to me at all, not even at the graveside. After the funeral we went back to my place and had a cuppa and something to eat. His daughter and the rest of his children went back to her place instead of mine. They only came to my place later.

Also, a strange scary thing happened a few days before Peter's funeral. The phone rang and I answered it, expecting it to be one of my many friends who had been ringing after Peter's death. It was a woman's voice on the other end, but one I didn't recognise. She said, "Is this Elly?" When I said it was, she continued, "It should have been you instead of Peter. You better watch your back at the funeral." I was quite frightened. I asked who was speaking, but the line was silent. I hung up.

This threat really threw me. I told the funeral people what had happened and they took it seriously. They kept a close watch on the people attending the funeral, and I kept my eyes open as well. I had to be on guard all the time, and couldn't really relax or focus properly on the funeral. Nothing happened. I figure Peter's children were behind it and had gotten one of their friends to make the call. They were probably trying to scare me, to get back at me for inheriting everything in Peter's will.

When Peter died I lost a lot of friends. Some people didn't think it right to be friends with a young widow. These friends saw us as a couple and we had always done everything together. It was not the same with only me.

I had my first paranormal experience a few months before my husband died. One night, in early hours, I saw my mother sitting at the end of the bed. She talked to me that night, saying everything would be ok and for me not to worry. In the morning I told my husband about the experience. He told me it was my dressing grown hanging up on the door. "Your mother wasn't here, you silly woman".

Later I understood why my mother came to me that night. She came to warn me about my husband's impending death.

I experienced six deaths in 16 years. Three of them were only 18 months apart. The hardest thing was that I was not there when any of them died. I never had a chance to tell them how I felt or to say goodbye to them. I never had a chance to tell them that I loved them.

How did I feel after all the deaths? When my sister died I felt guilty. It was my fault. I was not there for her when she was at her lowest point. I should have known what she'd been planning. I believe in my heart that if I had told my sister that I also was abused she'd still be alive today. We would have been able to help each other because we were so close to each other.

Again when my oldest brother died I believed it was my fault. I hadn't been there to help him. I'd let him down, like I'd let my sister down. My brother had asked me if he could come and stay with Peter and me for a while. If I'd let him stay he might not have gone to the beach that day.

With the deaths of my parents it was different. I was very close to my mother because of my cerebral palsy and all that I went though when I was young. My mother was my rock when I was growing up. She was there every time I needed her. When my mother died I felt that I lost that rock and I didn't know what to do without her. Dad's death was completely different. He was not there for me like my mother but he was still my dad. I had to be there for him. That's why I fought so much for what he wanted to do before he died and again regarding his funeral.

When my other brother died, I was not as close to him as my sister and brother were. I was shocked that I was not told earlier. When I found out where and how he was buried I was very upset. I went to see where he was buried and I was ashamed. He should never have been buried like that. If Mother was still alive when Paul died, he would never have been buried that way, she would have given him a good funeral and a headstone. I have promised myself to do something for my brother before I pass away.

I am going to write about one more death – that of the baby that I would have had if I had the choice to do so. My brother forced me to get rid of the baby by having an abortion at 12 weeks. I feel that it's important for me to write how I felt and feel about this situation. I felt that I had murdered the baby I was carrying and I had no control over my life. This baby would have been the only one I would have. Lately I've been thinking about this baby, wondering if it would have been a girl or a boy. Would he or she have had a disability? What would he or she look like? I can only ponder and yearn.

I never got to say goodbye to any of them...

Mother

I miss you very much and I wish that you were here with me. I need you. I do not know what to do now that I have brought out the past.

The hardest thing I've had to bear is to want my mother and know she's not there. My heart aches as I whisper, "I miss you Mum and want you". I know that God only takes the best and often ask myself why? Taking a grand person who meant so much. I'm sorry; I will not stop loving you until I die.

I can't cope with the feelings that I am going through. I can't talk to my husband about anything. I know you did not want me to marry my husband for reasons still unclear. I did not listen to you; I had to get away from everyone and everything.

Mother why did you have to die? I can't understand why you kept your illness away from me until it was too late. I am your daughter. I had a right to know. I wish that you were here to give me hugs and to tell me "what I'm going through will be alright".

I love you and you left me without saying goodbye. It hurts me that we never had time to say lasts words. My heart aches for you. You were my wonderful mother who gave me life and courage but most of all you gave me love. The tears in my eyes I can wipe away but the ache in my heart stays.

We had some good times and some bad. We laughed together and cried together. I sat up with you night after night waiting for the boys to come home.

Mother, I know that I promised you that I would take care of my brother but I broke that promise when he asked me if he could stay with me. I said no to him. I wish I had not said it and I regret that decision. I feel so guilty about it but Mother, I didn't know that he would drown.

You were there ready to help make things easier. You gave so much and took so little. Mother, one day soon I will be with you and we can talk about what I am going through when we are together.

Love you lots,

Elly

Helen

Why did you die? Why did you take those tablets? I knew what you were going through because I was going through the same thing. I will never understand why you did this.

I knew that the children were Dads. You didn't have to tell me. I made out I was asleep when Dad came into our room and got into your bed. I knew there was nobody else you were seeing. I knew you were in pain. I could see it on your face; you could not hide it like I did.

I think of you often in silence and I often speak your name. All I have are memories of you. The happy beautiful times we shared together are all gone but they will live in my heart forever.

They say life goes on. I know it's true, but it's not the same without you. To me your memory will never grow old because it's locked in my heart in letters of gold. There is a place in my heart that is yours alone: a part of our lives that no one else can own. To me the memories of you will never fade.

You did not let me say goodbye and it hurts so badly. There are so many things I wish I had said to you but nothing can express the way I feel. I loved you. And please remember that I always will. Until we are together again. I hope it will be soon Sis.

Elly

Dad

I am going to write this to you because I feel that I should write to you. I am going to tell you how I feel about what you have done. And how I feel about you.

Firstly I would like to say you have stuffed our family up. You had no right to do what you did. I also feel that if you had not abused my sister she would be still alive today. She would not have felt the way she did if you hadn't held on to her for all those years. She could not live any longer: that is why she felt that committing suicide would be a way out. She was only 38 years old. She had a lot of life to live. You have made me feel guilty over her death because she took my tablets when she died.

I also want you to know that I knew what you were doing to my sister. I saw you coming into our bedroom every night after you thought that everyone was asleep. I was still awake but I made out I was asleep. I saw you climb into her bed and even saw you having sex with her. I watched my sister's face and it showed that she hated what you were doing to her. I even knew that the boys were yours because there was nobody else in her life. You did not let her have friends, as you wanted her to yourself.

When the boys were born, you and my sister moved away to live together. You lived like a husband and wife instead of a father and daughter. You knew that it was wrong for you to do that but you kept doing it and she became pregnant again but she had an abortion because you were the father again. My sister lived like this all her life until she died.

I feel it is your fault for what I been through in some ways because to me, if you hadn't abused my sister, my brother may not have abused me. My brother used to say what was good for the old man was good for him. I don't know why you had to become an abuser. I don't know why you picked my sister. I can't understand why you did this. Mother and you had a good life and you had eight children together.

Now I will tell you how I feel about you. You are a bastard for what you have done to our family. We should have been a happy family. You and mother should have stayed together until she died. Mother never deserved what you did to her. You were my father and I loved you like a daughter should but I hate you for what you have done to my sister and to me. I will not forgive you for what you have done.

Elly

Michael

Why did you die the way you did? I miss you very much. My brother there is a space in my life which will never be filled. You were the best brother anyone could hope for. To me you were someone special. You always did your best.

Not a day goes by without thinking about you, wishing you could be still here. Tears still come to my eyes. All I have are memories and a picture of you.

I think about the good times we had together. We went away every Christmas time. We played together, laughed and fought together, but we loved each other no matter what.

There is a single wish, a silent prayer. If only you could be here. To hear your voice and see your smile is my dearest wish.

I don't think I can ever get over losing you; I deeply regret that promise I broke when you asked if you could stay with me and I said NO. But I could not know you would die the way you did.

My brother, you never gave me a chance to say goodbye. It hurts me so much. I will never understand why you went into the water that day. When we meet again you can tell me why.

Elly

Paul

I felt that I should write to you, to say how I felt about what happened to you. Also I'd like to say how I feel about you.

Firstly, I regret not going to your funeral but I could not face all the bull dust and the arguments among the family. It would have been different if Mum was alive; there would not been any arguments. That was one reason why I didn't go.

The other reason was that no one had told me where and when your funeral was. They didn't have the guts to tell me, as they knew if I did go I would have known how you were getting buried. I should have been told, as you were my brother as well as theirs. I did love you as a sister should've but I am sorry for not showing you how much I did. Also, I'm sorry I wasn't as close to you as I was with the others and even with Dad in some ways. You must have thought that I didn't love you or care about you but deep down I did in my own special way.

I am sorry that it has taken me this long to find out where you were buried. I feel very guilty about not finding out before. In a way, I wish I didn't find out, but then I could not live with myself if I didn't. I would have been wondering where you were for the rest of my life. When I finally found out where and how you were buried I was shocked and ashamed. I didn't expect that you would be buried the way you were. You should have been buried like the others. You have to believe me when I say that. Mum wouldn't have let you be buried the way you were.

I promise you one thing - our brother will pay for what he has done to you. I will make sure this happens. You were his brother and you deserved better. Brothers should love each other, not treat one another like dirt, which our brother has done. I will also promise you this: I will try my hardest to give you a headstone.

Elly

Peter

I miss you very much and I wish that you were still here with me. I need you more now than before.

I know now that you knew you were dying but you didn't want me to know because you didn't want me to worry about you. I was going through a rough patch with my health. You were very worried about me. You had told a few friends to watch out for me when you go. I can't understand why you told friends and not me. I was your wife. It really hurts that you didn't tell me how bad your heart was.

We had ups and downs in our marriage but you were there when I needed you the most and I was there for you. I wish that I was there at the end. When you needed me, I was not there for you. I wish I had stayed at the hospital but I didn't know how bad you were until it was too late. I am sorry that I was not there when you needed me the most. I will never forgive myself for that.

I was hurt when you left me the way you did. You did the same thing: you didn't wait for me to come and say to you that I LOVE YOU. That really hurts because now everyone that I have loved has gone from me.

If you did this because of the argument we had only days before you died, I am very sorry for not telling you earlier but I knew what your reaction would be. I wanted to keep it away from you forever but the nightmares were getting worse to cope with and I had to tell you about what happened to me when you asked. I could not live the way I have been living and that was in HELL. You called me a slut and a moll; you also told me I was no different to the rest of the family.

Those things hurt me but deep down I knew that you were right to say that. If I had told you about my brother you would not have let him in the house but you didn't know what he had on his mind when he came to stay. When you left us in the house for those hours, I knew what he wanted. I should have stopped him but then he took me back to my childhood and had his way again with me like before.

There is not a day goes by that I don't feel guilty about what has happened. I should have done something before it went too far but I didn't and I am paying for what I have done by losing you. If we never argued on that day you may not had the stress and you may still be with me today.

Now I have lost you forever. You were the only family I had. The promises I have made to you, I will not break them like I have before. I will keep them between you and me. They will come true and one day we will be happy again.

Do you know what is the hardest thing for me? It is the loneliness at night when I want to say something and you're not there. I miss the cuddle and you to say it will be all right.

I thought I would be able to cope with your death but I realise that it is very hard and no one understands what I am going through, unless they have lost a husband or a wife. Some people think I should be over your death and they think that I will commit suicide. I am going to prove them wrong. When you died I wished it were me instead of you because you were a good man. I did wrong all my life and I should have been the one to die. Still today I feel guilty about the argument. I feel I caused your death. No one will change my mind about this. I still think that it was my fault. The tears still come to my eyes and the ache is still in my heart. They say time will heal but neither time nor reason will change the way I feel. No one knows what I am going through when I cry myself to sleep.

Since your death I have tried my hardest to not argue with your children as I feel that you wouldn't like me to. It has been hard not to, with some of the things they have done since you have died. Remember that I will always love you no matter what and I know that you did love me. You never gave me a chance to say goodbye. There are so many things I wish I had said to you before you went. There is not a day goes by without thinking about you and wishing you were still with me. I miss you very much and I love you always.

Elly

Visiting Helen's grave

Peter's cemetery

Mum and Dad's cemetery

Michael's cemetery

Six

LIFE WITHOUT MY HUSBAND

When my husband died I felt that my world was falling apart. It seemed I'd lost all the people that I had loved most. I didn't know what to do about it. I started to lose weight from that day on. I was between twelve and fourteen stone and a size 16 depending on the make of the clothes I wore. Now I am only around eight and a half to nine stone and a size 12.

After my husband died, I went into my own little world because I didn't want to be hurt again. I felt safe in my home. I started to shut everyone out of my life by staying in my home and not going out at all. I didn't even answer the phone when it rang. I let it ring out, and then I would check the phone to see who it was. If I wanted to talk to them I would ring them back but most of the time I didn't. I just didn't want the hassle of my late husband's children, because I knew what they would be like. This was the only way that I could handle the situation of losing my husband. It was the last straw like the saying goes - "the one that broke the camel's back". The only thing I was worried about was the animals and I had to look after them like my husband would have if he were alive.

Arranging my husband's funeral was difficult. I knew what he wanted me to do when this day came, as he had told me a few weeks before. He didn't want to be buried with the other family members at the family plot. He wanted me to bury him where it was easy for me to go to. Before he died we both went to see the place where he wanted to be buried. His family didn't agree. I told them that this was their father's wish and that's where he was going to be buried whether they liked it or not. It was hard to say goodbye to him for the last time.

Another decision I had to make was about the two dogs and the cocky (cockatoo). The dogs were getting old; one was 17 years old and the other 14. We had had them both since they were 6 weeks old. They were part of the family. They had never been apart. They did everything together, slept together, played together and even ate together. They were mates. They did have their fights but the older one was always the boss.

I had to make a choice about the dogs because I didn't want the older one to die in the backyard, so after a lot of thinking I decided to put both down. So I asked a friend to come and take them both for me. When they came in the back door the younger one thought she was going for a walk but the older one knew that she was not coming back home. She looked at me with her sad eyes as if to say goodbye to me. It hurt me so much to do this because she was my husband's dog and she was one of the only things I had left of him.

I kept my husband's memory alive with pictures of us together framed around the house. I talk to his picture every day. We shared a lot together and the memories are treasures of the good times, the funny times, and the bad times. After he died I used to wake up early on a Sunday morning and would go out and pick some roses from the garden. I then took them to his grave, riding my scooter. This trip took around 30 minutes each way, and I stayed there for about an hour before I rode home again. I never missed a Sunday. His favourite roses were red, yellow, pink and white.

How was I going to go through life without my husband? I ended up ringing Lifeline to talk to someone about how I was feeling. The young lady who spoke at the other end was good. She listened to me for a couple of hours. Then she suggested I have some grief counselling.

She gave me a phone number to ring the next day. When I rang, I spoke to a woman and I explained what I was going through. She asked for my phone number so she could ring me after she spoke to her manager. When she rang me back she had arranged a taxi there and back home for me. I had an appointment with an unknown man. I didn't know what to expect from this appointment.

When I arrived I was not sure whether it was a good idea to discuss my concerns with a stranger. When it was time to be called in I was scared but I soon realised that all my fears were groundless.

I met with a man who was very nice. His room was uncluttered with a wooden desk and chairs. There was a picture of some kind on the wall. He asked me to sit down then he asked me questions about the deaths. I didn't think I would ever open up to a stranger but he was a good person and I knew I could open up to this man. Finally I was talking to him about all the deaths that I had been through, and how I wasn't coping at all. I could not hold back the tears any more. I am a person that doesn't cry a lot. I keep it all inside. But this stranger whom I had just met made it all come out. I could not stop crying. He was a very caring person and he knew what he was doing. I have never cried in front of anyone before this day. I have always put on a brave front.

This man could help me and he asked if he could come to where I lived because he could see the inconvenience I had getting to his office. It started every fortnight for some weeks then monthly. If I had not gone that day, I am not sure where I would be today. I recommend counselling to everyone that needs someone to talk to.

After my husband died I had the first of many operations. This surgery was on my back. I felt guilty because my husband had told me never to let any doctor touch any part of my back or spine. He was worried about me ending up in a wheelchair for the rest of my life. The MRI showed that I had to have an operation as soon as possible or I would not be able to walk at all. I had hardly any feeling in my body. I had no choice but to have the operation.

When I went into the hospital to have the operation I carried a picture of my husband in my bag. I took the picture out and said to the picture, "I am sorry but I need this operation". I was in hospital for a few weeks.

After a few months recovery, I had to have the same operation again as it appeared the first operation was not done correctly. I went into another hospital for this operation. It was better this time but my feeling in my legs and hands never came back. It was too late for that.

To Peter

This is one of my hardest letters I've ever had to write. I don't know how to start this letter to you. I know that I have to write to you about what I have been going through since I had my two operations. Also I want to explain why I had them. I want to tell you what I am feeling now that I know what the outcome is.

Firstly I would like to tell you that I know I have made another mistake in my life by having the operations. I should have listened to my husband once again. You told me never to have an operation on any part of my back, spine or neck. I am feeling so much guilt about the operations. I also feel that I have betrayed you by going behind your back.

Now I am going to tell you why I had the operations. The doctors told me I had no choice, I needed the operation. Also I had to try and regain my feelings so I could live a normal life again. That is why I did what I did. I can't turn back the clock. I wish I could but I can't. When I had to have the same operation over again, it was because I was starting to get worse again. I felt in myself that I had to have the operation again. I still feel guilty about both operations because I knew what you were thinking and I knew that you were scared about how I would cope without you if I couldn't look after myself.

Now I will tell you how I feel knowing what the outcome is. To me you should still be here with me, as I need you more than ever now. I am very scared of what is going to happen to me. I am worried that one day I will wake up and I will not be able to move. I put on a good front for people but really deep down I am not coping anymore. I do not know what I should do anymore. I have tried my hardest to do whatever I can but it is getting very hard.

Sometimes I feel that I would be better off dead but I wouldn't commit suicide like some people think I would. I feel that I have been punished for what I have done in my past. I knew the past would catch up with me one day. When I do become paralysed I can say to you that you were right once again.

I hope one day you will forgive me for what I have done. I am sorry that I still make mistakes. One day I will wake up to myself when it is too late.

Elly

A few months later I was having problems with my lower back. I could not sit or lay down much at all. The pain was like a knife stabbing all the time, which you could not pull out. The doctors thought it was to do with my cerebral palsy but I knew it wasn't. I had asked them for another test to be done. They put me on the waiting list, as it was nearly Christmas. I could not stand the pain I was having and I rang up and spoke to a woman and explained to her about what was happening. She rang around and spoke to the doctor who was looking after me. Then she rang me back and said that I needed to go in the hospital in a couple of days. They had to come back from their Christmas break early to operate on me. Then the operation came after that.

I had to have another operation. This time a few days before I was meant to go into hospital I woke up and I saw Mum standing by the door of my bedroom. She spoke to me and said, “Don’t worry everything will be fine and you will not suffer anymore”. Then she blew me a kiss and she left.

At that time I didn’t know why Mum had come. It made me think but I found out while I was in hospital. She had warned me that I would be having complications during and after my operation. My blood pressure dropped very low and I had a chest infection (pneumonia) and they could not find my pulse. They were worried about me. There were doctors and nurses looking after me 24/7. I could not remember the two days after my operation. I slept a lot in the earliest weeks.

After my husband died my brother Jack came back into my life again. He knew my husband was not here anymore to protect me. My brother wanted me to agree to let him look after his little sister again. I didn’t want this to happen to me because I knew if I allowed this to happen he would have the control over me like he always had. I didn’t want that scared little girl to come back.

About two years after my husband died, I wanted to try to meet someone for company. I decided to put an ad in the paper to see if I could find a male companion. A few men answered my ad. I liked the sound of one of the messages, so I decided I would contact him. We spoke on the phone a few times. He then asked me if he could come to my home. I thought it would be OK since I had spoken to him for a while. On the arranged night it was raining heavily and he was running late. When he arrived he had one thing on his mind. That was to have sex with me. I didn't want this but he raped me and left straight after.

I didn't know what to do. It happened on a Saturday night. I wanted to forget it ever happened. I could not sleep because I was scared that he would come back and do it again. I would not even sleep in the bed where it happened. On the Monday my counsellor rang me in the day. He knew something was wrong and he kept on asking me what was wrong. I finally told him what had happened and he convinced me to report this person to the police. We both went into town to report the rape. I had to give them details of everything that happened that night. The man involved was found and charged, but the case never went to court. It was his word against mine. The crown attorney did not believe there was enough evidence to get a conviction.

A few months later I met a person online though a game site, of which we were both members. We started to play the games together every time that we could. He would come on straight after work in the mornings until bedtime then before work next day. We couldn't get enough of each other. We spent hours and hours on line every day together. Then we started to get feelings for each other and we fell in love. He was the first person after my husband that I allowed in my life, who I loved. After a while I felt it was the right time and I took my wedding ring off. I knew that I did the right thing by doing this. I had not taken my wedding ring off my finger from the day I had married my husband until that day yet I felt it was the right thing to do.

Then after being with Brian for nearly 3 years things started to change and he was not the same person I fell in love with. He wouldn't come online and talk to me but, if he did, it was all hours of the day and night. I am not really sure what happened between us. He never discussed our relationship in detail. But I can say that he brought me out of my sadness. I will always love him no matter what he does.

After my husband's death, some other good things began happening. I knew they were messages from the spirit of my husband and mother. I often had people with me when these incidents occurred. The first was when I was on the phone to a friend and while I was speaking music started playing from a snow globe. Another time I was sitting around the table with three friends, and a clock timer that I never used went off three times without anyone touching it. Then I had a friend and her daughter staying with me for a few days. The clock in the spare room chimed the time that my husband died. Then I had a meeting with someone, and when she came to my house, a clock radio that my mother had given me (and that had never worked, from day one) started to play music then stopped. I felt these occurrences were all signs from my husband and mother to tell me that everything would be OK.

Around this time, I met a woman who began visiting my home. I had not known her at all before this. She looked at me and she said, “You have had a lot of trauma in your life”. I said, “Yes”, that this was true. This woman then started to tell me that what I’d suffered was all about the abuse. Then she told me about the deaths that had happened.

She even “spoke” to my husband. She warned me about another person that I was talking to on the Internet. Apparently this person was not a good person and she named him. No one knew who I was talking to online. From that day to this I never spoke to him again. I deleted him.

Then she told me things that only my husband and I knew about. She described an item in my house in much detail. When I went to see the item and how she described it, it was identical to what she had said. While my husband was "talking", my mother was trying to come though over the top of his voice. She also wanted to say something to me. I believe now that the visiting woman came to me that day to give me a message from my husband and my mother.

Since I lost my husband I have been to America twice. From a young age, I always wanted to go to America. I wanted to go to Disneyland to see Pooh Bear. I promised myself that if I had a chance I would go. I met a few friends though a game site and got to know them well. They lived in America and we would chat while we were playing games. From 2004, I chatted regularly with them. I told them one day I would be coming over to America. I told them I wanted to go to Disneyland.

They said I could stay with them while I was there. It was a good opportunity. I could also meet them at the same time. So I arranged to go over. The first trip I had to catch four planes. My friend had arranged more of our friends to meet me. They came from Texas, New York, Oklahoma, Pennsylvania and California just to meet me.

We went for a drive through the Amish Country. We saw their little school and watched how they plough their crops with cart and mules. They have their own shop where they sell homemade wares.

A few days after we went to see the Amish Country it was almost time for me to come back home. While I was on the plane, a man went to the Amish School in Pennsylvania where my friends had taken me a few days earlier. This man had three guns. He went into the one-room Amish schoolhouse intending to go on a shooting rampage. He shot ten girls and he killed five, aged between 6 and 13. Then he killed himself. All this happened while I was on the plane. I was glad that I didn't go there on the day of the shooting. But I was sad to hear about what had taken place.

We went to the Hershey's chocolate factory too. There were different kinds of chocolates. I have never seen so many in one place before. They had a car that you could go in for a tour, which told you the story of Hershey's chocolates.

I went on a wild weekend with the girls to a couple of hotels. They never thought I could be a wild person because I am normally shy. I showed the girls the real me when the wild side came out!

The next trip I went on was to stay with my friend in California for 2 weeks. She had arranged a 3-day pass for us to Disneyland. The hotel that we stayed in was across the street from the gates. On the first day we went on some rides: the Space Mountain, California Scream and the Twilight Zone Tower of Terror. They were terrifying rides but fun. While we were sitting, the High School Musical came to where we were and performed a concert. People were singing along with them. Some children were asked to help them with things. There were a lot of food places where you could sit and eat.

The next day we went I saw Pooh Bear and I had some pictures taken with Pooh. Other characters were also walking around Disneyland such as Dorothy and the Mad Hatter, Tigger and Goofy. We had a few more rides that day too.

The last day we were in Disneyland, we went shopping to buy gifts for friends and souvenirs for myself. We went on any rides we had missed. One was in a boat that fell down a mountain into water but you had to hold on to other people around their waist. It was too scary for me. I can understand when they say Disneyland is where dreams come true because my dreams did come true. I will have the memories in my heart for the rest of my life.

The next morning we had to drive back to my friend's place. It took us a few hours. Along the way there were restaurants called Denny's. We often stopped at one of Denny's to get a banana split. Their banana splits were huge compared to Australian ones.

When we got back we had a couple of days before we had to go to San Francisco. While we were in San Francisco we saw The Golden Gate Bridge, and a street called "the crookedest street in the world" which makes eight sharp turns in one block, and we drove down it. We then went to see China Town, and San Francisco Bay. We saw the cable car turntable at Powell and Market Streets, went to Fisherman's Wharf and Pier 39.

Later I went to stay with my other friend in Pennsylvania that I had stayed with the year before. I stayed with her and her husband for a fortnight. Some of my other friends came back to see me again. They stayed for a week with me. We had so many laughs and good times while they were there.

After our friends left the next morning we packed our bags to get ready to go to Canada. We wanted to see the Niagara Falls. We got up early to leave, as it was a long six-hour drive ahead.

After a while we arrived in New York State where half of the Niagara Falls was located. Then we went over to the Canadian side. I think the falls were better on that side. When we arrived there was a rainbow over the falls; it was beautiful to see. I have never seen anything like it before. You could feel the spray from the falls.

After coming home to Australia I knew there were some changes needed in my life. I had to make my own decisions, and I had to know where my money went. These changes were difficult, as my husband had helped before. I had no one to discuss anything with. I had to be careful how I spent the money. The bills came first then food. Sometimes I had nothing left in the pantry until the next fortnight. I also had to plan to cook for one instead of two.

Some of the strengths I've gained include making payments on bills alone, becoming independent, and moving house. It's been hard to pay the bills but I was determined to do whatever it took. This has made me independent. Moving house was most difficult because I had all the memories of my husband. I believe that my husband and my mother come to this house where I am living now.

My husband loved roses. He had every colour in the garden. He always went out in the morning and evenings to water them if needed. Then he would feel them all in case they were ready to drop their flowers. Peter never liked the flowers to fall on the ground; he use to say it was a waste of time if they did. Not very often he would bring some inside but when he did it was a special time.

When I moved house I brought some of his roses with me. They were pink yellow and red standard roses. Every year the first rose to flower is Peter's red rose. I believe that it appears first to give me a sign that Peter's watching over me.

I believe with all my heart that I would have been better off not being born. I would have not gone though what I have in my life. Sometimes when I'm going to sleep I wish that I wouldn't wake up in the morning. I don't deserve to be on this earth. I feel guilty about what I have done in my life. Going through everything I have. The way things have turned out. Then I look at the achievements I have made: marriage, the blessing of meeting good people, travelling, my writing of this book to assist other people with their traumas, and so much more.

I still feel guilty about being a burden on my family when I was young. Another worry is that I am left with only family members whom I do not feel close to. With my marriage, I feel guilty that I couldn't conceive a child because of what I went though in my life. I know that my husband would have liked a child but I couldn't give him one. Another guilt I have is not being accepted as equal in my husband's family like all the others were.

Due to the restraints of my cerebral palsy, I see myself being alone in the future because I don't see anyone accepting the way I am. I have to learn to be alone the rest of my life. I can't stand the loneliness I am feeling since my husband died. I have been sleeping with my head on my husband's pillow. I feel close to him by doing this. I have tried my hardest not to think about everything but sometimes it overwhelms me. There is the loneliness at night when you want to say something to the person that you are close to and they're not there or when it's cold I want to cuddle into a warm body. When things go wrong I wish you were here to say it's going to be all right.

IN TRUTH I HAVE LIVED MY LIFE TO MY BEST ABILITY
AND HAVE FOUND I MUST ACCEPT MANY
DISAPPOINTMENTS
BUT MUST ALWAYS ATTAIN THE BEST SOLUTION

Amish Country, Pennsylvania

Amish school, Nickel Mine, Pennsylvania where 5 children were killed by a gunman 2 October 2006

My American vacation
San Francisco, Disneyland, Niagara Falls

MY POEMS

I began to write poems when I started to remember what had happened in my life. It was one way that I could handle it. I began to put pen to paper to write down how I felt. I started to write poems in about 1983, after I was married. I came up with ideas by thinking about everything in my life and what life should be like. Then I decided to put these ideas on to paper. I rewrote them until the poems were as I thought they should be.

When I Was Ten

Why when I was ten
and still an innocent child
as you decided to abuse me.
Did you never ever stop
and think just what
you were doing to me?
Did you never consider how
I felt about what you were doing to me?
Did my cries and screams
not get through to you?
I always asked you to stop.
I didn't want you touching me.
I hated you using my body
the way you did.
I cried and cried for you to stop
but it was a hopeless plea.
You were so much stronger than me
and though I tried to get away
it was never to be.

No matter what you do,
I will never ever forgive you
for what you put me through.
Abusing me and causing me
so much pain and misery
that my life never felt like mine.

I Don't Want To

I don't want to
Can't you hear me?
I know I have to do
what you tell me to
because you're my older brother
and I'm just your little sister
Besides, you scare me
with your threats.
Why does this give pleasure?
Touching me the way you do
I am a small, scared
defenceless child.
My body
yells "NO"
I try to scream out but my mouth
won't work.
No words come out.
And I know that I mustn't tell anyone.
No, I will never tell.
My heart is racing so fast
and all my body is tense.
No one will come
to this small girl's defence.
You knew your secret was safe
Thirty years later it's coming
back to haunt me.
You are my nightmare brother
I feel I am in hell
every time I remember what you did.
Did you ever think what this
was doing to me?
What right did you have?
You took away my childhood.

The Don't Tell

The don't tell
came to live
in me
when I was
only ten

The don't tell
had for me
great power
that took
me over
years and years

The don't tell
made me so
I couldn't tell.
Inside me
I had
to scream and yell

The don't tell
always was
around.
He made sure
my voice
I would never find

The don't tell
stayed and stayed
with me
but he shrank
by a level

The don't tell
was scared
and on the run
but he fought
to stop me
having any fun

Over My Head

Am I in way over my head?
Has the water run too deep?
Will the memory of you haunt me
when I try to go to sleep?

Is it right to be this happy?
I can't love anyone any more.
Should I stay, or get away from you
By swimming to the shore?

All I know is the ecstasy
You've brought into my soul,
My heart feels like a 'tidal wave'
That's just begun to roll.

Your love has never rescued me
yet I'll never go back down.
If your love is the ocean,
Then I think I want to drown.

You Meant So Much to Us

MUM

You meant so much to all of us
You were special and that's no lie
You brightened up the darkest day
And the cloudiest sky

Your smile alone warmed many hearts
Your laugh was like music to the ear
I would give absolutely anything
To have you standing here

Not a day passes
When you're not on my mind
Though the hurt will ease in time
Your love we will never forget

A Broken Heart

Long black hair
big brown eyes
behind her smile
the truth lies.

She cries herself
to sleep at night
she wishes things were
simple
plain - black and white.

But things are hard
for her to understand
for she is not in control
and matters are out of her
hands.

No one can help her
not even her friends
Sometimes she wants
her life to just end.

The pain is hurting her
it's killing her soul.
Her heart is now broken
when it used to be whole.

She wonders why
this happened to her.
She wants things back
as they once were.
Maybe one day
she'll learn to forgive.
But for right now
she doesn't want to live

He hurt her so much
the one that she loved.
Now she prays for help
from the good Lord above.

But no one would guess
All of the pain
that's built up inside her
slowly making her insane

Soon she will have had
about all she can take.
She just couldn't handle
another heartbreak.

She cuts her arm
to relieve the pain
She wants it to end
To hit a big vein.

She knows that it's
not the only way out?
But lately it's all
she can think about.

Appendix

Information About Cerebral Palsy

Cerebral Palsy (CP) is a disorder affecting movement control, which results from damage to part of the brain. The term cerebral palsy is used when a problem has occurred to the developing brain, usually before birth.

CEREBRAL - refers to the brain.

PALSY- means weakness or paralysis or lack of muscle control.

The brain determines everything we do. Different parts of the brain control the movement of muscles and other parts of the body. With CP, there is damage to, or the lack of development of, one or more areas to the brain.

People with CP can have problems such as weakness, stiffness, clumsiness, and difficulty coordinating simple movements, shakiness and difficulty with balance. These problems can range from mild to severe. In mild cerebral palsy, a person may be slightly clumsy in one arm or leg and the problem may be barely noticeable. In severe CP, the person may have the whole body affected. Each person with CP will be affected in different ways depending on the harshness of the brain damage and the area of the brain affected.

Certain words are used to describe parts of the body affected:

HEMIPLEGIA – is when the leg and arm on one side of the body are affected.

DIPLEGIA – refers to both legs affected significantly more than the arms.

QUADRIPLEGIA - both arms and legs affected, the muscles of the trunk, face and mouth can also be affected.

Cerebral palsy is a permanent, lifelong disability. However with early treatment and careful management, it is possible, in many instances, to modify the effects of the disability and enable each person to achieve the optimum degree of independence and to live with an acceptable quality of life.

What are the different types of cerebral palsy?

There are several different types of cerebral palsy; they can be put into categories. The most common one is

SPASTIC CEREBRAL PALSY - stiffness or tightness of muscles because the message to the muscles is sent incorrectly through the damaged part of the brain.

When people without CP perform a movement, some groups of muscles become tighter and other groups of relax. In people with Spastic Cerebral Palsy, both groups of muscles become tighter. This makes movement difficult or even impossible.

ATHETOID CEREBRAL PALSY - causes involuntary unpredictable movements. This involuntary movement is present even at rest and is often most noticeable when the person moves. Children with athetoid CP often have very weak muscles or feel floppy when carried.

ATAXIC CEREBRAL PALSY – is the least common type of cerebral palsy. Ataxic is the word used for unsteady shaky movement or tremor. People with Ataxic CP also have trouble keeping their balance.

MIXED TYPES - when several of these types of CP are combined.

What is the cause of cerebral palsy?

There are many different causes for CP. The risk is greater in babies born preterm and with low birth weight. The reason for this remains unclear. Cerebral palsy may occur as a result of problems associated with preterm birth or may indicate an injury has occurred during the pregnancy causing the baby to be born early. Around 90% of cerebral palsy occurs during pregnancy delivery and the first month of life.

In some cases damage to the brain may occur due to:

- the baby not growing at the correct rate during the pregnancy
- the mother being exposed to certain infections at the early stages of her pregnancy, causing a lack of oxygen to the baby (particularly during birth)

- the infant developing a severe infection (meningitis or encephalitis) shortly after birth

What other difficulties do people with cerebral palsy have?

There are seven other difficulties that may occur with people who have cerebral palsy:

- Disorders of hearing
- Epilepsy – also recurring seizures (fits).
- Disorder of eyesight - such as squints or other visual problems.
- Intellectual disability and learning difficulties - People with CP vary widely in their intellectual and learning capabilities. Some will show the same intellectual capabilities as other people in spite of their physical difficulties. Others will have some degree of intellectual disability, ranging from mild to very significant.
- Perceptual difficulties - Perception is making sense of information gained through the senses. This enables people to do things such as move around obstacles, judge the size and shape of objects, and understand how lines are connected to form letters. People with CP can have problems with perception as the brain may have difficulty interpreting the messages it receives from the senses.
- Speech difficulties - The muscles of the mouth may be affected, and some people with CP may find talking

difficult. Some people may be mildly affected while others may not be able to say any words at all. People who cannot speak clearly may use a communication board or electronic communication device.

- Eating and drinking difficulties - Cerebral palsy may affect the muscles that open and close the mouth and move the lips and the tongue. Chewing and swallowing certain foods can be difficult.

Do people with cerebral palsy get better?

Cerebral palsy is a life-long condition. Generally the weakness, stiffness or unwanted movement remain throughout the person's life. People with CP live with it all their lives. It is important for children who have CP to receive support from an early age to ensure they have every opportunity to reach their full potential. Many people with cerebral palsy are healthy and live to old age. Those people with more severe forms of CP may have a lot of health problems that result in a shortened life span. There is no cure for cerebral palsy.

Can people with cerebral palsy lead a normal life?

People with mild cerebral palsy often need no additional support to undertake the activities that most people enjoy. On the other hand, people with severe cerebral palsy may need assistance to eat their meals, shower and dress and go to the toilet. They may also need special equipment to communicate or move around such as wheelchairs or walkers. These days new technology has made a huge difference to people with cerebral palsy. They can use computers to surf the net, email friends, apply for jobs and work in paid employment. Computers allow people with disabilities to operate everyday appliances such as TVs, videos, stereos, and air conditioners. Today people with cerebral palsy have a wide range of skills, qualifications and experiences. Some of them have abilities that enable them to work at an entry level while others have tertiary qualifications such as TAFE certificates, diplomas and university degrees.

In conclusion it is important to focus on what the person with cerebral palsy can do and the ways they can maximise their achievements and to keep in mind that their physical appearance may not indicate their intellectual or cognitive abilities.

www.ingramcontent.com/pod-product-compliance
Ingram Content Group UK Ltd.
Pitfield, Milton Keynes, MK11 3LW, UK
UKHW020129250726
13967UKWH00002B/555

9 781446 115909